THE
ASSASSIN
AND THE
DEER

THE ASSASSIN AND THE DEER

A NOVEL

DIANE WEYER

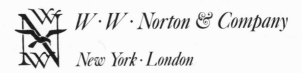

W·W·Norton & Company

New York·London

First Edition

The text of this book is composed in Times Roman with display type set in Egyptian
and Caslon 540. Composition and manufacturing by The Maple-Vail Book Manufacturing Group. Book design by Marjorie J. Flock.

Library of Congress Cataloging-in-Publication Data

Weyer, Diane.
   The assassin and the deer / by Diane Weyer.
      p.   cm.
   I. Title.
PS3573.E984A8 1989
813'.54—dc19   88–22551

ISBN 0-393-02594-2

W. W. Norton & Company, Inc. 500 Fifth Avenue, New York, N.Y. 10110
W. W. Norton & Company Ltd., 37 Great Russell Street, London WC1B 3NU

1 2 3 4 5 6 7 8 9 0

This book is dedicated to Dora, who never doubted, and to the memory of Irene, who helped in spite of her doubts.

CONTENTS

THE
ASSASSIN
AND THE
DEER

MOUNTAINS ARE FOR MURDER

IT ALL STARTED when Paul fell off the mountain. When I was holding him and trying to hang on until they could get a rope to us, with 2,000 feet of empty air below us, it was then I saw the saw-through karabiner hanging from his harness, only it wasn't his karabiner, it was mine. He'd borrowed it. I was supposed to have been the one to fall, not the young university student whose mop of brown curls was slowly turning red. Wet, sticky red. Only if I had been the one who fell, there would have been no one to rescue me. No one else on the climb has the training I've had. So—somebody tried to murder me on that beautiful clear, clean mountain. But instead I held the broken body of my bouncy, irrepressible, young climbing partner.

One eye was half-open and the blood was seeping into it, slowly obliterating the blue with red, but I had no free hand to wipe his face.

We were climbing in the Andes, the frozen sentinels of the Western Hemisphere towering above us, oblivious of the tiny crawlings of men—we were on the side of a minor peak at the base of one of the main cordilleras. The peak still stretched 19,000 feet above the sea, which we could have seen as a thin blue line on the horizon had there not been storm clouds over the coast. But our mountain was many miles inland and the sun glinted off the snow above us almost painfully. I knew, from previous expeditions, the snow fields, the two vast glaciers, and the final summit where the mountain shrugged unimaginable tons of ice and snow aside to thrust rock pinnacles hundreds of feet into the soft underbelly of the sky. But that morning we had turned off below the permanent snows to where a quarter of the mountain had sheared away in some ancient upheaval, to where the rock face dropped straight down with barely a pebble sticking out to mar its symmetry.

There was a route across near the top, which Paul was leading, looking rather like a mobile lichen inching his way over the rock. I was belaying him and he had a couple of good runners in. I can still feel how warm and solid the rock behind my back felt, as I sat there in the sun, paying out the rope for Paul. He is slim and quick and moved with the confidence of a youth who doesn't believe he can die. I remember looking out to see if the clouds had cleared away from the coast yet. When I looked back Paul had stopped moving. I watched, trying to picture what the difficulty was. It looked as if the crack line he was following ended and he appeared to be considering coming down a few feet to a lower traverse that looked as if it might have possibilities. Then he was hanging by his hands. Then he was off. I braced to take the impact, hauling back hard on the rope. The figure eight the rope ran through was a new one. So was the rope. But suddenly the rope went slack and we watched in stunned disbelief as he fell free while the rope came hissing back down through the runners.

If Paul had fallen ten feet before he did, there'd have been nothing to stop him for 2,000 feet. But he'd gotten just beyond the completely sheer drop. He fell about 15 feet before hitting a rib of rock, then he was sliding along it at an appalling rate. He came to a wrenching halt, with his left arm wedged between two rocks at a hideous angle, but holding him for a moment. Slightly below, and maybe 90 or a hundred feet across the cliff face from us. Somehow he twisted around and got a hold with his right hand. His left arm slipped out of the rocks and hung at his side.

The other members of our party were frantically trying to work out a route that would take them around the top of the cliff to where they could try and drop a rope to Paul, but it was obviously hopeless. There was no way in the world he could hold on that long with one hand, in his condition. He couldn't tie onto a rope, either, without help.

I could see the death knowledge in his eyes even from where I was. I've seen it so many times. . . . Paul is 22. He has a girl he's going to marry just as soon as he can save up a little money. We've climbed together on so many mountains—Paul warbling "and they scraped her up like strawberry jam!" whenever I was struggling with a difficult spot.

Maybe there had been too many deaths on my last job, I don't know—maybe just that I knew he was so young, he hadn't believed he could die until then.

Whatever, I wasn't consciously aware of having untied and yanked off my belaying gloves until I heard someone yelling at me that I was insane, that I didn't have a snowflake's chance in hell. I started across. I guess my conscious mind switched off and my subconscious took over, like that old Korean guy teaches us to do in emergencies, since your subconscious can operate much faster and more effectively than you can yourself by thinking. Anyway, this time it happened by itself, without my trying. I have a horrible recollection of my aware mind curled up in a fetal position, mewling in abject terror somewhere in the back of my head. I hardly saw half the tiny flaws in the rock that my fingers and feet kept reaching for. Momentum, balance, and luck—a lot of luck—sent me flying across the cliff towards Paul.

Then I slammed into the rock shelf I'd been aiming for and the worst stretch was past. Felt like I'd caved all my ribs in, but clutching a rock with my legs dangling over a 2,000-foot drop was no place to stop and inspect damage, and Paul was somehow still hanging on by one hand. I don't remember hauling myself up or covering the remaining 40 feet or so between us, but I must have because then I was beside him, with one arm around his waist and the other holding us, stuck well back in a crack in a good solid, bombproof, fist-jam. With a little work, I got myself wedged across and could take some of Paul's weight against my side, which relieved my arm somewhat but made my leg start shaking almost immediately. My other leg hung free, there wasn't anything to brace it against or stand on. Paul tried to grin and I tried to also, but if mine looked anything like his, it wasn't very successful.

There was nothing more I could do but hang on and pray the others could get a rope to us in time. I don't know whether prayer helps or not, but it did give me something to do besides wonder how far I'd splatter if I fell. Have you ever tried NOT to think about something? Fortunately my mathematical abilities weren't up to working out how high 120 pounds of blood and meat, well, about 270 if I included Paul, would splash when dropped the 1,500 feet or so that I estimated it was to the next ledge.

It seemed like several centuries before the end of the rope brushed my arm. Then I discovered Paul was unconscious. I had no free hand to tie either of us on with. In fact I was virtually unable to move. Finally, I realized that if I "lay back" almost horizontally, I could brace with my shoulders and so free my arm and hand. It proved to be more difficult in practice than in theory—

every muscle was rigid and any movement was pure, unadulterated agony—and I nearly dropped both of us in the process. Fortunately, someone in the group had realized that tying on might be difficult and the end of the rope was knotted in a loop with a karabiner hung off it. Tying a secure knot one-handed under such circumstances would have been impossible. As it was, it took me several lifetimes to open the karabiner and fasten it around one strap of Paul's harness. Then I tugged the rope three times to signal them to haul him up, trying to will them to pull him up slowly and gently—he was only attached at one point and was unconscious—he'd hit every rock on the way and could wind up with a broken neck. Then I stopped thinking and just held on.

Eventually the rope came back down and I was hauled up, to collapse, retching, at the top of the cliff. People were congratulating me and fussing over me, but I hardly heard them because I suddenly realized I'd worked the karabiner under Paul's harness because only half of his karabiner was there. That was what had broken, not the rope. The sudden jerk of the rope under such tension must've snapped it, except that karabiners don't break. The screwgate might come loose if you're careless, but they don't just break. Besides, I could see it hanging there, in my mind's eye, and there was a smooth cut three-quarters of the way across. A deliberate cut. As I said, it was mine. Paul had borrowed it because his had some grit caught in the threads. I remembered being slightly annoyed when I found it borrowed and had to dig a spare out of my pack.

I staggered up and tried to get a look at the remaining piece, but it was no longer on Paul's harness—either fallen off as he was pulled up or someone had removed it while everyone's attention was on me gagging my guts up.

I stumbled down the mountain in a daze while the others took turns carrying Paul down. A quick examination by Mark had shown a splinter of bone sticking out of his shoulder, and it looked as if there was another break a couple of inches down his upper arm. He looked terrible. The jouncing on the way down brought him to, screaming with pain. It took a long time to get off that mountain. Fortunately, we keep morphine in the climbing hut, where we'd left the cars, so he had some relief on the way to the hospital.

I was in no shape to drive, so I sat in the back of Mark's car with Paul's head on my lap. Once I was sure he would live, I let myself start to think about the implications of the accident and nearly started gagging again. My cover had been broken by someone who very nearly succeeded in killing me. I felt very cold and very alone. I looked at the lines of agony on Paul's face—he was a kid still, no conceivable threat to anyone. A kid who'd come terribly close to dying because of me, not that he would ever know that. He thinks I'm just a somewhat eccentric freelance journalist who likes to spend her free time in the mountains. His pain was simply a mistake—and someone was going to pay for that mistake. But Bobby taught me long ago that emotion is for afterwards—at the time it only clouds the thinking. So I tried to put aside the jumble of feelings that were paralyzing me and began to consider it as strictly an intellectual problem.

My climbing and hiking have been a refuge from the shadow world I work in. Now a shadow had tracked me up into the mountains. To have tried to kill me this way, the shadow was almost certainly a member of the climbing club. There was a new member who'd been with us on the climb and who'd only joined a week or so ago, according to Mark. I'd not met him before that morning. But I had no proof and someone could have been suspicious of me for some time and only recently had those suspicions confirmed. I know of too many people who would be willing to wait a long time if they could be sure of killing me. My shadow could be anyone, even Mark, though I didn't like that thought. The only person I could be certain it wasn't, was lying with the blood oozing from his head onto my slacks.

I looked out the window at the mountains, away from Paul, and tried to think back—had anyone tried to loan him their karabiner instead? Or tried to interfere in any way with his taking mine? Couldn't say for sure. But a pro wouldn't have risked giving himself away by doing so. He would just hope Paul never put sufficient strain on it to break it.

That train of thought ended when we reached the hospital. Once we had Paul safely ensconced in a private room, Mark insisted on taking me to his small, tidy apartment after calling friends and asking them to collect my car from the climbing hut. He insisted I come in for a drink and a meal while we waited for my car. I agreed, as Blade was away, and wouldn't be waiting for me. Mark is a big, blond, easy-going Humanities professor. Perhaps the closest thing I have to a friend, outside of the Organization. Paul is my climbing partner, but we share no other interests. It's almost impossible to have friends outside of the Organization; it's too easy to slip in your cover story or be asked awkward questions as to how you got those ''funny-shaped scars'' or something—too much effort to be worth it. But Mark never asks questions. He's passionately interested in primitive art, loves museums, and shares my tastes in music. Since he prefers men when it comes to bedpartners, there are no awkward questions about my scars since he never sees me minus clothes. Perhaps his homosexual preferences are why he virtually never asks personal questions. Whatever, I enjoy his company, but I had other things on my mind so I left immediately after eating, pleading exhaustion.

Drove down to Headquarters, automatically using the patterns Bobby taught me long ago that would allow me to spot anyone tailing me. Satisfied no one was, I turned up the narrow track that leads into the compound. The floodlights showed low buildings set at pleasing angles in a grove of trees a quarter of a mile ahead, looking like toys in a child's play set. But no child's toys would have electronic gadgets that can monitor a gnat flying across the driveway—height above ground, size, weight and shape down to the last millimeter, speed, flight pattern and projected flight path. I'm told there used to be barbed wire, patrol dogs and the lot, but that was gone long before my time. Now there is nothing to spoil the beauty of the place—and it does have some lovely old trees and gardens.

I waited at the gate for the night man to come let me in. His doberman, Suzy, came over and stuck her head in the window, asking to be petted. I did so, before being let in, while feeding her one of the dog biscuits I keep in the glove compartment for her. Headquarters is the one place I feel completely safe, no matter what. Nothing short of a direct nuclear hit is ever going to give anyone inside any gray hairs. It felt very good to drive in. Home may be where the heart is, but it's also where you can relax and know that no one can kill you.

I would have to be leery of my house until after I found out who was trying to kill me. If they knew where I climbed, I had to assume they also knew where I lived. My house has a few gadgets in it too, but nothing like Headquarters, nor does it have the armament Headquarters has. Just as well Blade was away, this way I didn't have to go near my house, and there could be no risk to him either. Nonetheless, I wished my Afghani rebel was around— I'd missed him and had been disappointed when I found he'd been sent back to Afghanistan for a couple of weeks. I parked the car and headed for the room I use whenever I have to stay at Headquarters for any reason.

I tried to sleep but kept seeing that sawed-off karabiner. Finally I quit trying, sat up and started reviewing everything I knew that might be pertinent—not much. First, the other climbers: who was it that had yelled at me and tried to stop me? Mark? I thought so but couldn't be positive. Even so, had he really tried to stop me? I wasn't paying attention just then. He had acted very concerned about me afterward—but so had the other three, and one of them had tried to kill me. Probably, anyway. I was getting nowhere on that track. Mmm. Whoever did it had to have recognized me somehow. By my climbing style? Many climbers have their own distinctive styles of climbing. I can recognize any of our club's members by the way they climb, and Paul calls my style "idiot class 1," so it must be easily recognizable. Someone might have recognized me that way. But I'd only climbed on two jobs in the past year, and I couldn't think of any loose ends in either one. Besides, a sawed-through karabiner seemed an odd choice. Could've been months before I ever put enough strain on it to break it. And even then there was no guarantee, either that the rope would also break, or that I would fall far enough to kill myself. Other methods would have been far more certain. Of course, a climbing accident would never be questioned. Was that important?

I was getting nowhere fast, so I quit worrying the problem and thought about what needed to be done for Paul instead. I'd better make some arrangement between my bank and the hospital in the morning, early. He couldn't begin to afford what that arm was going to need, and I knew he didn't have insurance either, because we'd talked about the high cost of medical insurance not long before. Paul's always broke, like a lot of students. Didn't seem reasonable to risk my neck and then let his arm stay a mess for lack of money when I've got plenty. But I'd have to figure some way so he wouldn't realize I was paying his bills, or he'd walk out as soon as he could stand up. Mmm. Decided to ask the Boss to let me use our legal section.

My thoughts wandered off to some of the climbs we'd done together. The time he'd had a fight with a girlfriend and called me at two A.M. suggesting a three day climb starting as soon as possible—we were in the car two hours later. A good climb. I climbed long before I joined the Organization, but it's become far more important to me since. I need to get up where the wind blows clean and cold and I can only die through my own carelessness or just sheer bad luck, not because someone wants me dead. And rocks can't deliberately torture people. Of course, you can get hurt climbing, but no one wants you to hurt. I once placed a runner without double checking, and when I slipped a few feet further up, it came out. I slid 60 feet and ripped a gash right to the bone and the length of my thigh in the process. Made an ugly scar but I don't mind it like I do some others I have, even if they aren't as nasty looking.

I woke up later, shaking and sweat-soaked from a nightmare I couldn't remember. Five A.M. Couldn't see the Boss before eight, so I showered off the sweat and combed and coiled my waist-length black mane into two tight coils on either side of my head. Decided to skip makeup—not at 5 o'clock in the bloody morning. Besides, no makeup could really erase the dark circles under my eyes—or remove the red rims which looked god-awful around my green eyes.

Went down to the training section. Bobby was there already—wonder when he sleeps, or maybe he doesn't need to. He looked around as I came in and raised a hand in greeting. Small, pale, with sandy hair, and made out of steel cord and razor blades, Bobby is one of the top experts in the world on death and the myriad ways to cause it. Our chief trainer—and I guess my closest friend in the Organization next to Blade.

I chose a pistol and spent an hour doing some of the worst shooting I've ever done in my life. Finally Bobby came over carrying two steaming mugs of coffee, and nearly dropped them when he saw my target.

"Jesus Fucking Christ, Tessa! WHAT are . . . YOU shot that . . . that . . . that disgrace?!"

I grabbed the coffee before it all wound up on the floor and glared. I sipped it cautiously—it's usually half rum and very strong when Bobby makes it—as he walked down for a closer look at my last target. He brought the paper "man" back with him. I already knew how badly I'd shot.

"Was this for fun?" He looked hopeful, then shook his head, "Nope, guess not from the look on your mug. Okay, so what's wrong? You never shot this bad even when you was first train'n."

"Forget it." I sipped my coffee and tried to look unconcerned.

"Forgit it!! How'n hell am I suppos'd ta 'forgit it'? Train'n you is my job—thought I'd finished long ago but now you do this! What'm I suppos'd ta do when the Boss wants your record or asks if you're cleared? Lie through me teeth?? Then whose fault is it, you get killed? Huh?" He looked furious.

So was I for a moment though I knew perfectly well he was right. But I couldn't tell him what had me shaky either. Friend or no, security is too tight for that sort of talk. The Boss was the only one I could tell that someone had broken my carefully built and cherished cover. I didn't wish to lie to Bobby—I have to all the time whenever I'm outside—so I said nothing. We walked over to his work bench and sat in silence, me feeling more alone and more frightened than I have in centuries, and Bobby fuming. When I set my mug down he picked up my hand and looked at the back of it. So did I. The veins stood out like cords and showed blue through skin that looked thin and dry. Old-looking. But 34 isn't old and my hands didn't look like that a couple of months ago. Exhaustion ages. So does too much tension for too long. Tension also makes for lousy shooting, though I'd never had my shooting affected before. 'Course I'd never had my cover broken before either.

"You gonna take some time off for a while? Like a long while?"

"Hope so, but, I kinda doubt I'm gonna get much chance to for a while yet."

"Ain't seen you around for quite some time—when you get back?"

"Yesterday. Went climbing right after I got out of debriefing, though."

"How long was you gone?"

I knew what he was leading up to so I just said "Too long."

He laid my hand back in my lap and didn't say anything. He didn't need to. We sat in silence awhile before he suddenly asked me the one question no one asks in the Organization—"How'd you come here anyway?"

I was too surprised to answer for a moment—guess it never occurred to me that he might ever have been curious even. Nearly said, "None of your bloody business!," but then I saw the look on his face and realized again just how much he does care about me. Not many people do—my occupation doesn't exactly lend itself to close relationships. So I told him.

"I was born in French Guinea. My mother claimed to be French but the neighborhood children soon corrected me about that. She was the result of a Portuguese sailor and an Indonesian whore. I inherited my face and temple-priestess body from her, as well as my permanent tan. My father was a sandy-haired, shambling Englishman, a bank clerk. A man who drank too much and wasn't very nice to live with. One Monday morning he was gone. For a while the police notified my mother every time they fished a body out of the river. Then they stopped bothering. At the end of the year, a minor discrepancy was found in the bank's figures.

"My mother was a small, shy woman who never doubted that

the world was brutal and unfair, and the world did nothing to change that belief. Life isn't easy anywhere for a woman with no training, of dubious background, and alone except for a five-year-old child to care for. In West Africa it was virtually impossible. Fortunately for us, an Indian merchant took pity on her and set her up as his mistress. Suddenly there was food again, and nice clothes, and I started school. Uncle Jawa (I never knew his real name— Jawa was as close as my mother could come to pronouncing it) was a large fat man with thick fingers who laughed a lot and liked children. We had seven years. I guess they were the only really happy ones I've been given.

"You remember when French Guinea went Communist in 1958?" Bobby nodded. "Suddenly, brutally, the country collapsed into chaos. Men in heavy dark clothes, totally unsuited to the African heat, appeared on the street, speaking a language no one understood. Some said it was Russian; turned out it was Czechoslovakian. The men never moved without guns. Anyone who didn't do as the strangers ordered was whipped and beaten, or shot. Not understanding was not an excuse. Sometimes even those who tried to please the newcomers were killed. It was a time of terror.

"For eight months Uncle Jawa was allowed to go on running his store. Then a soldier came in and found nothing he wanted to take. He shot Uncle Jawa in the stomach. Uncle Jawa was still alive the next day when they came into our living quarters behind the store. My mother hid me in a closet but I ran out screaming when they kicked her in her belly and stripped her clothes off. A huge man with tiny gray eyes in a flat scarred face grabbed me and shoved me at the others to hold. They laughed and knocked me down again and again as they took their turns raping my mother. The second time around the big man with the tiny grey eyes sawed off her breasts with his bayonet. Her screams of utter agony seemed to amuse him. She was still alive when they got tired of their sport. She called on God, but what she tried to beg of Him I don't know, because the man who'd sawed her breasts off smashed the heel of his boot into her mouth and she couldn't speak through the broken bones and splintered teeth. The last man to leave turned and shot Uncle Jawa through the head as an afterthought.''

I sat, remembering the horror, until Bobby gently shook my shoulder. I sighed and went on.

''Why they left me alive and unharmed, I have no idea. Certainly many children were raped and killed during those years. But I was left to cry as the last of my mother's life leaked away. I was still crying the next day when an African woman passing outside heard my sobs and came in and dragged me away from the already-rotting corpses. The sun was bright outside when she forced my head up to see it and wiped away the last tears I ever cried with the hem of her brightly colored skirt. No one could afford another mouth to feed in those years, but she was kind and couldn't bear to leave a child to die. She shared a piece of dried fish with me, the only food she had, and insisted I eat it. Then she scooped water out of a puddle beside the road for me to drink. Finally she took me to a French mission station. They took me in. I stayed there for three years, until just after my fifteenth birthday. The missionaries helped anyone who was hurt, regardless of who they were, and they taught me a great deal about practical nursing in those years.

''Perhaps I was beginning to believe in their faith a little as well. I was still determined that somehow I was going to kill the people who killed my mother and Uncle Jawa, but you can't be around that much kindness and concern for human life without some of it rubbing off. Until the night the Communists burned the mission. The Sisters were raped or their long robes set on fire, and they were chased and jeered until they died. They skinned Father Bernard alive. I will hear his screams until I die. I recognized two of the men who led the murder party—we'd treated their wounds not two months before.

"Overlooked in the confusion, I hid in a ditch in the dark and watched everyone else be murdered. Then I ran through the African night farther and faster than I have ever run before or since.

"That was the start of years of wandering, of learning to live in a world where no one cared whether I did or not, of always being hungry, of learning to steal and to beg. No one would hire a filthy, scrawny girl who spoke only a smattering of English. Five years of the roughest survival lessons in the world. Then a stolen wallet yielded unbelievable riches, nearly $300.00, which allowed me to get out of West Africa. I wound up in London, where I learned to dress and speak properly, while working a variety of menial jobs—working instead of begging and stealing—such an incredible difference.

"Four years later I had enough money to move on to New York. Not an easy city for a foreigner who didn't know anyone, but I managed and after a bit moved on again. I kept moving and wound up in Mexico eventually, working as a receptionist at the Mayan ruins at Chichen Itza—in the Yucatan peninsula. Well, not at the ruins really, at the Mayaland Hotel, 'bout a mile away on the main road to Merida.

"I was two weeks short of my 26th birthday when I killed the man who had cut off my mother's breasts.

"I still remember the soft breeze as I walked down 65th Street in Merida, window shopping, on my day off work. There was a big limousine stopped in a traffic snarl—and I saw him. In the back seat. His features had been burned into my mind with all the hate and fear a 12-year-old can feel. It was him, though the years had added grey streaks to his hair and a series of chins below his original one. Then the limousine pulled away, leaving me stunned.

"Until then my plans for revenge had been vague daydreams

that had no basis in anything besides my hate. Fourteen years is a long time, maybe my need for revenge was beginning to fade, then I saw him only a few feet away from me, on the opposite side of the world from where I thought he was. The next hours passed somehow—I have no memory of them. I'd read in the papers about a youth rally to be held that week in Merida. The headlines had denounced it as Communist-organized. Later that afternoon I went to the library and dug through all the recent papers. When I left, I knew the route the parade would take, that it would be held in two days time, and that there would be bodyguards for the Havana contingent of Youth for Peace. I didn't know then that the man I wanted was "an outside advisor" and one of the ones to be guarded. I hoped he might be one of the bodyguards. Of course, I couldn't be sure the man had anything to do with the rally, or the Cubans, but it seemed a possibility, and the only one I had. The best news for me was that all the visiting dignitaries, bodyguards, etc., would drive out to visit the ruins at Chichen Itza after the rally. With luck my mother's murderer would be delivered to my doorstep, so to speak. That night was spent pacing my tiny efficiency apartment in the back of the hotel and planning, or trying to. Seeing him die a thousand different deaths at my hands. Eventually I eliminated all but the simplest.

"I said I was sick the next day, which wasn't far from the truth anyway, went back to Merida to the bank, drew out my savings and bought myself a high-powered hunting rifle and 500 rounds of ammunition. In England it would have been impossible, in Mexico an extra $50.00 ensured no questions. What little money I had left went into the gas tank of my ancient Ford. Then I drove out of town, back toward Chichen Itza, until I found a deserted field with no houses in sight. I spent that day and 400 rounds of ammunition learning the gun and its capabilities as well as my own. I'd done some shooting before, but never with a weapon like that. Then I went back to the hotel and tried to sleep—unsuccessfully. My shoulders and arms felt as if they'd been hanging on to a jack hammer all day. An hour's soak in a tub as hot as I could stand it and a handful of aspirin helped, but I still couldn't sleep. I kept seeing my mother's final hours over and over again until the sky began to lighten and I gave up trying to rest.

"It never occurred to me that there would be any sort of security for the rally and the visit to the ruins, just as it didn't occur to me to plan any sort of escape. I didn't think beyond shooting the man. I guess I didn't care much.

"How many times have you told me that no matter how good a police or other security force is, they can't watch everyone?! All they can do is check for known troublemakers, keep an eye on any suspicious looking sorts, and generally make their presence obvious. They're pretty helpless against an unknown sniper, especially one who doesn't care if she escapes or not.

"I didn't know anything about all that then, of course, but I did know that a young woman wearing a bright orange dress and driving a battered old car wouldn't look like much of a threat. No one asked me why I had a raincoat on the seat beside me on a bright sunny day. I parked in the small car-park just past the drink and souvenir stands opposite the entrance to the ruins, having come early to be sure of finding a parking space along the main road. I wandered around the ruins and drank innumerable soft drinks so as not to draw attention to myself. The morning dragged in slow motion. I was terrified someone would discover the rifle, but I didn't want to be conspicuous by sitting in the car for hours either. Now, the thought of how much I had left to chance that day is appalling.

"Gradually, the ruins filled up with tourists. Cameras clicked and children chased each other up and down the steps of the temples. You know what, Bobby? I can't remember feeling anything, not fear, not excitement, not hate. I felt nothing and watched the people oohing and ahhing over the carvings on the temples. Finally, policemen barricaded the road to traffic. I went back to my car, opening the door and leaning on it after sliding the gun over beside me. The only bad moment was when the line of cars came into sight and I couldn't see the man I'd come to kill. Then, I saw him sitting in the back of the second limousine, talking to the man beside him. As the car drew abreast, I simply picked up the rifle and shot him. No one saw the rifle until after his face blew apart. I just stood there, couldn't believe I'd really done it, while police fought their way through hysterical tourists and snapped a pair of handcuffs over my wrists. I never even thought to drop the rifle and run or anything—shock, I guess. Well, I paid for that bit of unbelievable stupidity.

"My memory of the next 48 hours is pretty vague. I know I was beaten repeatedly during questioning. Beaten but not crippled, fortunately. But it hurt more than I'd have believed possible.

"The last time I was dragged out of my cell and down the corridor, I was flung through the door in front of a man I hadn't seen before. He didn't do anything, so after a moment I sat up. To try to stand, which I doubt I could have anyway, would've been inviting the guards to knock me down again. I was afraid to look up for fear of being hit, so I kept my eyes on his shoes—expensive shoes. The cloth of his trouser legs looked far too expensive to belong to any policeman either. I sneaked a look up in time to see a mild-looking, middle-aged man handing a hundred dollar bill to each guard. The guards went out, closing the door deferentially.

"My mind went blank. None of my acquaintances had money to throw away even if they'd known how to reach me—or wanted to. And I'd never seen this man before in my life. Nothing made sense anymore, least of all that he was squatting down, looking into my face as he spoke, saying something like, '. . . hurt you. Get up. I won't hurt you. But I want you to tell me what you've been refusing to tell those goons for the past two days. Don't be afraid. You've been very brave to hold out so long, and your friends will never know. If you answer truthfully, I'll get you out of here.'

"He spoke gently, in the sort of voice you use when talking to frightened children—or mental defectives.

"The police had demanded over and over that I tell them what the name of my group was, how many members, where did they hide, etc. I'd not answered simply because they wouldn't have believed me. Even to myself the truth was beginning to sound unreal—how could I possibly have done it alone, with no training? Now this man with the gentle voice was offering me hope if I would tell him what I couldn't because there wasn't anything to tell. Strangely enough, I never doubted his offer of help. I remember wailing, 'That's the whole trouble!! There ISN'T anything to tell!'

"He looked at me for a long moment as I sat on the cold, filthy floor, covered in blood and bruises and dirt. Finally, he stood up and lifted me onto one of the two chairs in the room. He sat on the other.

" 'You know, I'm inclined to believe you're telling the truth.' He looked as if he couldn't believe what he'd said. Then he sighed and went on, 'Suppose you start at the beginning and explain just how you happened to kill Laktovan and have nothing to tell.'

" 'Laktovan?' I asked.

"The man looked at me in utter astonishment. 'You don't even KNOW who you killed!!'

"I told him I'd never known the man's name.

"There was another long pause while he discarded several things he seemed about to say before he finally asked, 'Why did you kill him? Why did you kill a man whose name you didn't even know? Why Laktovan for God's sake?'

"He sounded angry, but somehow I felt positive he was still

willing to help me. Suddenly, something snapped inside and I was
telling him what I had never spoken of to another human being,
not even the nuns—telling of my mother's death and the man who
killed her.

"He got me out of hell. Ten minutes and several thousand
dollars later he half carried me out to his car. My rescuer took me
home and handed me over to his young blond Swedish wife. She
gave a shriek of utter horror, then ministered to me very effi-
ciently. For two day I did nothing but sleep, eat, and spend hours
in a hot tub soaking the pain out of the bruises and swellings. No
two people could've been kinder, but they refused to answer any
questions, or even tell me their names.

"The third day, the woman, still smiling as sweetly as ever,
plunged a hypodermic needle into my arm. When I woke up I was
inside Headquarters, though of course I didn't know that, on a
hospital bed, with a big Negro doctor prodding my eyeball with
his finger, say'n, 'She's com'n 'round now. Hummph, must be a
lot stronger than she looks—some dummy gave her twice the dose
she should've had, but she's throwing it extremely quickly.'

"So—here I am. You know all the rest—the tests 'n everything. You were there when I met the Boss too, 'n when he told
me the Organization had been going to kill Laktovan only I'd
beaten them to it. And how their contact in Merida found out where
I was jailed, rescued me and hung onto me until I was fit to ship
out to Headquarters. I remember you watching me very closely
when you took me in to see the Boss—figure I was gonna faint or
something? Been a long time since I've really paid any attention
to anything but the Boss's personality, but I must admit I nearly
threw up when I saw his face and hands!

"All I could see was his physical presence and I could only
just control my stomach. I think I managed to keep from turning
green as I looked at that horribly scarred and drooping left eye and

the deep trough that ends where his ear should have been. Then he put out his hand to shake mine and I nearly threw up. God! Only three fingers left and they can't flex. And that big hole in his palm. No fingernails on either hand and his left hand has some fingers that can't move. . . . I've never seen the damage that keeps him in a wheelchair, and I don't want to.''

Bobby grunted agreement and that pulled me back to the fact that it was morning and time to get moving. I sighed and said, ''Speaking of the Boss—I've got to get over and talk to him. See you later, okay?''

Bobby smiled a little and said, ''Ok. I'll save some coffee for you. . . . Thank you for tell'n me.'' He looked like he wanted to say something more so I left quickly.

I asked to see the Boss as soon as possible and his secretary sent me straight in. The Boss waved me to a seat without looking up. I sat down and looked at him quietly—if he wasn't ready to see me yet, there was good reason for it—he never kept people waiting just to show his power. The wheelchair squeaked slightly as he held a sheaf of papers in his twisted, grotesque hands. He was approaching 60, but 40 years of constant pain had aged him beyond his calendar years. The portrait facing his desk was the only spot of life in the room. Everything else was grey metal and bare walls. Not even a carpet relieved it—his atrophied feet couldn't feel a carpet, and it would have impeded the movement of the wheelchair. But the soft smile of the woman in the painting warmed the room and her eyes, the eyes of a poet, or a visionary, were constant reminders of what the decisions made in that room were made to protect. No other painting would ever join that one. The woman was long dead, and his crippled hands would never use a paintbrush again.

I think that portrait is part of why I trust him so totally—I'd trust anyone the woman in that painting would marry. And she had been his wife, a member of the French Resistance in World War II, until she was caught by the Gestapo. He tried to rescue her but something went wrong—all he had time to do was give her his own suicide pill. It was three more weeks before he was rescued, a couple of weeks too long for him to ever walk, or paint, again. What was left to him was a brilliant tactical mind and a passionate hatred of anyone who deliberately hurts people for their own pleasure.

Those two things were, I think, what caused him to be selected to run the Watchdog Organization. When the World Council for Human Rights finally decided they had to have a clandestine side to protect their field workers, they needed someone who knew all about killing and terrorism but who still had a soul and who truly cared about human beings—not the easiest combination to find, especially as that person also had to have the ability to put together a large intelligence network and oversee the creation of a Wet Work (that euphemism being borrowed from the CIA) section made up of similarly motivated people who were also extremely competent. The Boss had created the Watchdog Organization almost single-handedly.

I pulled myself back to the present as he laid aside the papers he'd been reading and spoke to me.

"Good morning, Tessa. I was going to ask you to come in today but you seem to be here already." His eyebrows rose, or rather, the one which can, rose in question of my unexpected presence. People usually see the Boss when he asks for them, but not otherwise. I wondered at his comment about sending for me but knew he'd tell me when he was ready—meanwhile . . .

"Someone tried to kill me."

The Boss blinked once.

"Yesterday, when I was climbing." The Boss's one mobile eyebrow shot up. My cover having been broken and all that that could imply hung between us. Finally he asked what had happened and I told him.

He watched me in silence when I finished. Then he steepled his nailless fingers and sighed, "Any ideas who or how?"

"Not really. Considering the method, it almost has to be someone in the climbing club. They wouldn't have had to be on the actual climb yesterday, but I think it probable as they would've preferred to switch karabiners on me as late as possible. Far less chance of my noticing it after I'd gone over my gear than before. There were four besides Paul and myself. I tend to prefer a man who joined us only a couple of weeks ago. Or . . . Mark, who's been a friend for a long time. I would rather not think it was him but he does know me better than any other outsider does."

"I should imagine we can discount him. A possibility, of course, but I'm more interested in this new member." He punched a buzzer and his secretary scurried in to get down name and description. He told her to start a check and give it top priority. It was typical of him not to question me about the other two who were on the climb. If I didn't consider them real possibilities, he would assume they weren't.

I asked him about asking the legal section to tell me how to handle paying Paul's bills and he agreed.

"All right. We'll leave that for now and see what the files can turn up. I think perhaps we should also send one or two people over to check your house for any signs of tampering or surveillance, just to be on the safe side. Meanwhile, how would you like to go to Belize for a while?"

I had a bad feeling the Boss wasn't suggesting a vacation for my health. Belize is my second home and I have family there— not a nice thought if I was supposed to work there.

The Boss pulled his wheelchair closer to his desk and said, "There have been numerous disappearances of important people, especially scientists, over the past years, as I'm sure you are fully aware. Most, of course, wind up in Moscow being wrung out for anything of value. However, there has recently been a sudden increase in 'short-term' unexplained absences of people from a great many walks of life. Our Intelligence Department has been curious and keeping track as much as possible ever since one of our men happened to be tracing someone and the computer he was using gave him about 30 similar cases as references, all within the past year and all from Freeport, Grand Bahama." He looked up and asked, "What do you know about Freeport?"

"Not much, playground for the wealthy, sun and sand and all that, but mostly casinos and luxury hotels."

"Yes, casinos. Virtually all of the 30 disappearances the computer turned up happened near or inside three major casinos. To cut a very long story short, two months of hard digging has turned up a most unpleasant sideline of the KGB's. Basically, all three casinos are partially owned by a Cuban who poses as a native Bahamanian. He was chosen as a young man, partly because he can pass as Negro, and he was given intensive training, both in Havana and Moscow, before being sent to the Bahamas in the guise of a native-born Bahamanian whose family had moved to the United States, etc. Needless to say, there was indeed such a family, who were killed in a car crash, all except for the boy who went to an orphanage. Also needless to say, the real Bahamanian has disappeared and no one is likely to question the man who took his place and name. Such 'sleepers' are a common story to all of us I'm afraid.

"Recently this 'sleeper,' by the name of Jedson, Ronald Jedson, has been activated, after being given control of three casinos, through a complex of cover companies, and been set to removing people targeted by the KGB. These unfortunates are always people of some importance in government or industry, important but not too prominent, people who have no close family ties or close friendships—and who gamble regularly.''

The Boss saw my look and nodded, ''Yes, wrung out completely, then killed, and substitutes sent back in their place. Some apparently to gather information, but most to cause disruption whenever possible. Incidentally, many of the recent leaks of sensitive and embarrassing information to the United States press have been the work of these substitutes. Well, the list of damage caused is a long one but most of it really doesn't concern us directly, although our intelligence people have passed on the information they've uncovered to the various agencies which have been infiltrated. Our concern is rather closer to home I'm afraid.

''As I know you're aware, the World Council for Human Rights, as well as the other human rights organizations, are becoming more and more effective. In doing so, we've managed to antagonize the KGB as well as a number of other people. So, they have apparently decided to try to influence our areas of concern, to make us concentrate primarily on the right-wing totalitarian governments such as the one in Guatemala and ignore the left-wing ones such as those in Nicaragua and Cuba.''

Seeing as I'm in charge of our Latin American and Caribbean section, that was hitting much too close for comfort and I sat up, literally as well as figuratively.

''How? Or should I say, who?''

''That is being taken care of. All you need to know is that several people in the communications department were involved.''

Oh God. The implications of a mole, or moles apparently, in the middle of our communications network made me want to throw up.

''Go on.''

''It has been decided that Jedson cannot be allowed to continue his operations. We could simply expose the situation to the Bahamanian government and get his casinos closed down. But only a very few casino employees are involved in Jedson's end of things, and it would cost the Bahamanian government a considerable revenue loss, not to mention the loss of jobs, etc. More to the point, Jedson would simply appear again under another name somewhere else in a year or so.

"Therefore, after considerable discussion, it has been decided to terminate Jedson."

"Considerable discussion" must've been the understatement of the year. This was a straight, out-and-out assassination, and the World Council for Human Rights cannot approve of assassinations, and the Watchdog Organization normally believes in killing only in self-defense or in retaliation for assassinations of our own people. For one thing, political assassinations very seldom really achieve much as the assassinated leader immediately becomes a martyr and a new leader promptly steps into his shoes. But this was a bit different—there must be no one groomed to take Jedson's place or they never would have decided to kill him. The story still felt incomplete somehow. I looked at the Boss for a long moment and finally asked, "What else?"

"What do you refer to?" The Boss isn't exactly someone who telegraphs his thoughts at any time, but he was *too* still and I knew I'd scored.

"You've left out something. If you are going to ask me to kill him, which I assume is where this conversation is going, there must be more to it than what you've told me so far." He blinked and finally sighed.

"Unfortunately you are correct. I hoped you wouldn't ask as I did not wish to alarm you unnecessarily."

"I'd be even more alarmed if we just started bumping off people out of spite. Besides, I have enough to be alarmed about already, maybe they'll cancel each other out."

The Boss did not smile. Instead he sighed again and handed me the folder of papers he'd been reading when I came in. I glanced through them quickly—mostly World Council memos, a few maps, a couple of eye-witness atrocity reports. Then I saw it. A transcribed conversation between the president of the World Council and the Boss in reference to several recent jobs done by us. I suddenly didn't think I wanted to know. The Watchdog Organization is a very tightly kept secret—only three people in the World Council even know we exist. The thought of Moscow knowing about us, and worse, connecting us to the World Council. . . . Asking was painful.

"Who knows?"

"Only Jedson so far. Plus the woman who passed this stuff on of course, but she's being interrogated right now. The KGB apparently is allowing Jedson to run the substitutes after they are in place. They, or rather the people they are impersonating, are all gamblers who go to Freeport regularly, so their pattern of gambling is simply continued and their information passed to Jedson who then passes it on to his masters. This batch of photocopies was reduced to a microfilm and smuggled out of the Communications Center at the end of the month. It was passed to Jedson two days ago. Normally he would have sent it on to Moscow by now. However, he is taking a vacation in Belize as of yesterday, talking about opening a casino there too, and so has not yet sent these on to Moscow. The microfilm was recovered from his home last night. We cannot be certain that he reads all he passes on, but he has the equipment in his bedroom, so we must assume that to be the case.

"Once he returns to Freeport he will, of course, find the microfilm missing. What will happen after that, we can only guess. But it has been decided that it is best if he never returns."

"So it's gotta be Belize."

"Yes."

Shit! My stomach hurt and I suddenly wished I smoked, just to have something to do besides wanting to be elsewhere. "Why me? I mean, plan it, sure, but Christ, I'm known from one end of Belize to the other—even the Immigration people greet me by name!!" I swallowed hard. I'd never balked at a job before, but this was different. "Isn't there any one else who can do it?"

"According to our information, Jedson will be returning to the Bahamas on the first of March. That only gives us 15 days. This is insufficient time to plan and carry out an assassination for someone who knows nothing about the place. You should be able to do it fairly easily, I would assume."

"Except for being found out afterwards. Plan it, of course. But doing it, in that place, with my cover already broken by someone is a different matter." I took a deep breath and stated the obvious. "Whoever knows where I climb very likely knows of my connection with Belize." Then I finally stated the real problem. "I have family there."

The Boss looked at me for a long moment. "No one else is free. There are simply too many things breaking in too many corners of the world at once. There's no one I can pull off of anything else without risking a great many lives." He sighed, "I know you're long overdue a rest. You may believe it or not, but I do keep track of such things." That surprised me.

I wondered briefly whose lives would be risked if I didn't risk mine this time, then wished I hadn't thought it. The Boss knew exactly what was involved for all of us. If he said I was the one to go, then I would have to. But I didn't have to like it. I nodded my acceptance of the situation and he handed me a paper.

"Here's Jedson's itinerary in Belize. Look it over and see if you have any ideas. Come back at 4 o'clock."

I was dismissed and I knew the Boss's mind was already elsewhere, but I remained seated and spoke my mind on a related matter.

"Boss, what you just said about being short of people—have you decided who's gonna be the new African Section head?"

He looked up, faintly annoyed—it wasn't really any of my business, but I had been the one he'd sent in to clean up the mess and bring back the bodies. "No, not yet."

Well, now or never, so I plunged ahead. "War's ready to be promoted."

"War?"

"Sorry, none of us can pronounce his tribal name so Bobby christened him the Zulu Warrior and it got shortened to War. The guy who came in from the riots in Basutoland, about seven-and-a-half-feet tall with a shaved head except for three strips of hair."

"Ah, yes. I was unaware of his new name. A rather appropriate one, I believe, from what his reports indicate." He paused and watched a spider working near the ceiling—at least that's where he seemed to be looking. "You feel he is ready to become a section head?"

"Yes, I do. I know he hasn't been with us all that long, but he's been working in the field for years before we picked him up."

"You are aware that it is not our policy to assign people of the same ethnic origins to that section, so as to reduce the possibilities of regional or tribal loyalties conflicting with what may be best for the area overall?"

"Yes. But War knows more about such problems than most of us do. Remember, his mother was Matabele and his father was Zulu, and she taught him to hate his father so much that he tried to kill him. When he failed, his father took him in and tried to teach him to hate his mother's people. Neither tribe will ever really trust him. He's passionate about breaking down tribal hatreds and building up viable African nations instead."

I plunged ahead before the Boss could order me out of his office, "Look, I know I'm poking my nose in where it doesn't belong, but I know War, and he'll never be happy anywhere but Africa. He's brilliant and can handle the responsibility. Let him try it—you can always transfer him later if it doesn't work—but give him a chance. After all, what have you got to lose? There's no one else ready to take over—Christ, there's hardly anybody *left* there now above the rank of clerk!"

"I'm aware of the death toll." (I most sincerely wished I could take back that last comment—I knew the Boss felt all deaths as his responsibility.) "And I will give your suggestion a try, although I fail to see that it is any of your concern. I believe you have enough concerns of your own at the moment without looking for more."

I was definitely dismissed now so I got up to go, but then I wondered, "Do the Brits know about Jedson?"

"Information isn't certain." Oh.

I took Jedson's itinerary and what little else we had on file on him and left. Went around to the cafeteria for an early lunch. Like the rest of Headquarters, the cafeteria was designed with individuals in mind and no expense spared. The food was always excellent, but I haven't a clue what I ate, could've been sawdust for all I know.

I sat in a chair set by itself overlooking the grounds, and started to read Jedson's file, pushing thoughts of War and the carnage I'd cleared up half a world away out of my head. Not that I knew why I'd decided to speak up about War either, but I'd felt for some time that his place was in Africa, no matter what the Organization's customs were. And he was a friend.

Oh well, back to Jedson and how to kill him.

When I finished eating, I walked around the grounds and down the stream for an hour or so, thinking. One of Jedson's appearances would be at a beating of the retreat at Airport Camp. The

British Forces in Belize were changing regiments as they did every six months. I'd been to several retreats and up to the camp on a number of social occasions as well. It would be an ideal place to do the job. As long as I wasn't actually seen with the gun in my hand, no one would ever suspect a female guest in a long evening dress and high heels of being the assassin. The rifle I could take through in the car. The parking lot was between the Officers' Mess and the parade grounds. There would be the inevitable cocktail party in the mess first, then we would stroll out to the parade grounds to hear the retreat itself. There were some trees just before the parade ground and there were never any decent lights there. As long as I could keep from being too closely escorted out, I could stop at the car on some pretext and get my gun.

A full-length skirt and a stole should do the trick since the lighting would be very poor anyhow. And security would be lax during the retreat.

With luck I could get a seat in the back row near the trees and away from anyone I knew. I could always plead the need for a toilet part way through, if I had to. There were usually three long rows of seats. Picking out Jedson at that range would be pathetically easy. Once into the trees, I could do the job and simply rejoin everyone as they were milling around after the shooting. The gun I could retrieve from the grounds later, if necessary even after driving out the gate. I could pull into one of the airport's back roads and come back into camp that way. I'd take working clothes along in the car. I've retrieved things, including people, from under the noses of guards and sentries and wasn't worried about that. An easy set-up, all in all. Then I realized the snag. The Brits would be blamed. Cuba would have a field day with it. I supposed it was too easy not to have a snag. So much for that idea. I mulled over the rest of the list but didn't see anything I liked. San Pedro's hotels 'n beach were too public and there was the risk of some innocent tourist getting shot. Likewise, with Jedson's overnight at the Fort George Hotel in Belize City.

Finally wandered back inside and wound up down in the training section. Found Bobby in the armory, cleaning weapons. He looked up and wiped the sweat out of his eyes, leaving a black smudge all across his forehead, as he said, "Good, you're just in time ta make yourself useful. Me cup's empty."

I made us coffee, half rum for him, straight for me. He handed me a pistol to clean and we talked guns for a bit. Then Bobby gnawed his lip a couple of times and finally spoke his mind.

"The grapevine has it you're off on a job again. Awful soon, ain't it? Thought you just got back yesterday."

"Yeah, but vacation time can wait awhile yet." Not true, but I had to say something.

"No. It can't. Not when you've been operational for seven weeks straight this last time 'n no proper break 'fore that either." He looked at me very seriously and I could see the worry in his eyes. Damn it.

"You keep'n tabs on me?"

"Don't need to. You look like the ass-end of a vulture at the moment. 'N I'll be nice and not mention your shooting earlier. But someth'n's wrong."

I tried to look as if nothing was bothering me. A waste of time, Bobby knows me far too well. He sighed and let the matter go. "Okay, okay. 'Nuff yap for now, you came here to think, not talk." My jaw must've dropped 'cause he grinned and said, "Don't look so surprised. You always go for a walk first, then come here when you're work'n out a job. You're like me, you think best with a weapon in your hand. Cleaning guns is relax'n. There's plenty that need doing."

I'd never realized I had such a set routine before. Set routines are disgustingly fatal in this kind of work. I wondered what other routines I had that I wasn't aware of—and if maybe that was how the shadow had tracked me to the climbing club. Nasty thought. Finished cleaning an SLR and started on another. Wondered how many life-affecting decisions I'd made while sitting on that bench watching Bobby's grimy hands working, with incredible delicacy, on the various instruments of death he loves so much. I let my mind drift. Eventually, I looked at my watch and realized I barely had time to get over to the Boss's by four o'clock. Hadn't realized it was anywhere near so late. But I knew how I was going to kill Jedson. And I'd decided, though I hadn't been consciously thinking about him, that Mark was not the one who'd tried to kill me. Right or wrong, that decision was made and I felt better. I dumped the SLR I'd been working on in Bobby's lap and chugged the last of my cold coffee.

He grinned, "Thought you was gonna wear out that barrel 'fore you got whatever you was figur'n figured! You been rubb'n that same spot for the past twenty minutes!"

I banged the door shut on any further comments.

The Boss didn't look up when his secretary waved me in, so I sat down in the swivel chair in front of his desk. He was reading the last page of a thick file heavily stamped in red. I tilted my chair back and watched the spider still at work on the ceiling until he spoke.

"We apparently have nothing on your new climber. The computer drew a total blank. He seems to have materialized out of thin air, so I should imagine he's our man. One of the boys is out trying to get a photo of him now. Hopefully, he'll match up with someone we have on file."

I said "Thanks," and meant it, while hoping that whoever was trying to track him down and photograph him was being damn careful—if he was our man, he wouldn't want his photo taken.

"Now then, have you come up with any ideas regarding Jedson's termination?'' (''Termination'' always sounds like such a euphemism to me. Not that the Boss hides behind words—he's killed too, years ago, but there's nothing wrong with his memory. ''Termination'' still sounds peculiar to me.)

''Yep. Didn't like any of that list. Get so used to thinking in such terms that the obvious answer took awhile to see. Jedson'll be visiting in Belmopan, the capital. Unlike the rest of the world, Belizeans have never gone in for assassinating their politicians. As a result, nobody worries about security. Well, not what we would call security anyway. Even the prime minister lives in an ordinary house like anyone else. Jedson will be staying in a private house with no special security unless he brings bodyguards with him. And Belmopan is perfect—small population, individual single-story houses mostly, separated by yards, lots of trees and hedges. The whole place is connected up by deep concrete monsoon drains.''

The Boss didn't exactly smile, but his face shifted momentarily. ''Okay. I'll leave it to you, you know more about what your problems will be than anyone else. Think on it some more tonight and tomorrow we'll ask the computer.''

I grimaced—rather have the Boss's opinion than that overgrown tinker toy's any day.

''Assume you'll be leaving tomorrow afternoon. Get a good night's sleep.'' I must've looked surprised—the Boss isn't known for wasting breath on pleasantries—because he added, ''That's an order.''

Oh.

I drove home. My house means a lot to me, my retreat from the world I suppose. As I walked in I looked at it as if seeing it for the first time. Perhaps because I was no longer sure if it was safe anymore. I knew the techs had pronounced it untouched and clean, but anyone who knew where I climbed probably knew where I lived.

I went upstairs to shower and change. My bedroom is large and luxurious in the extreme. A fantasy bedroom but real, and mine. My bed is enormous and round, with a built-in curving headboard that has everything one could possibly want at hand. Tape deck and tapes, a tiny fridge for wine and cheeses, a coffee percolator and a choice of Kenyan, Colombian or Costa Rican coffee, a small select library, mostly Oriental and Persian volumes. My alarm clock sits between a pair of erotic African carvings I picked up in Rhodesia a couple of years ago.

What invariably draws one's attention is the enormous round ceiling mirror directly over the bed. This is supplemented by another mirror curving around nearly half the bed at mattress level and extending up to meet the ceiling one. This whole unit occupies one corner of the room and is one of the main reasons I bought the house. Rumor has it that the aging playboy who had it installed died of a heart attack. Whatever he died of, his spinster sister was only too glad to sell it. The corner opposite is taken up by a huge fireplace flanked by two easy chairs. A totally impractical pale rose carpet does double-duty as a wall-to-wall yoga pad. Of course I don't suppose any carpet is really meant to be walked on in muddy climbing boots. Anyway, it matches my sheets.

I showered leisurely, trying to relax, and then called the hospital. They wouldn't let me talk to Paul yet, said he couldn't be disturbed. Finally, got hold of his doctor who said Paul would be in a cast for at least four or five months. I'd go crazy if I had to live in a cast that long. Wondered how Paul would survive—better than being dead, I guess. I still felt like it was my fault Paul had been hurt. Assassins shouldn't have friends.

I put on an Al Stewart tape and spent an hour doing yoga exercises trying to shut everything but the music out of my mind. The notes slid along each other like liquid crystals. I have a super sound system—when I first started working for the Organization and knew I'd have some money, I went to our chief mechanic, who is a sound equipment buff, and asked him to get me the sort of set-up he'd choose for himself, money no consideration. The results are Bose speakers in the bedroom, living room and kitchen; a Linn Sondek turntable, Niam amps, a Teac reel-to-reel tape deck and two Neal cassette decks, one in the living room and one in the bedroom. Since he'd particularly drooled over the Teac reel-to-reel, I bought him one as a thank you for all the purchasing and installation. Final bill was a bit over $30,000.00.

Gave up on the yoga, couldn't concentrate. Mixed myself a very strong screwdriver instead. Wished Blade were here—the house seemed awfully empty without his slightly larger-than-life presence. Not that he lived here, but he was usually around whenever I was home between assignments. I missed Blade. The damn house echoed him everywhere and I kept half expecting him to touch my face as he walked through the room. Except, of course, he wasn't in the room. He was in Afghanistan, maybe even with his child-wife. Blade had showed me a picture of her and their two little boys. A sweet, serious-looking girl, whom Blade had never met before their wedding night, although they had been betrothed as children. And now she had nothing but his name, and his children to raise. Not that she was alone, she lived with his parents and both families were wealthy—but still . . . the original bird in the gilded cage. But she'd been born and raised in the gilded cage and couldn't imagine any other life. Blade was adamant that his children would see the Western world and learn English as he had, though at first he was only going to send his sons abroad. I convinced him that he must also give any daughters he might have that choice too.

No, I really couldn't begrudge her the few days out of the year that her husband visited her. I just wished it didn't have to be tonight. If Blade really loved her I suppose I would feel jealous, but I knew there was only one woman for him and that was me— no matter what obligations he had. Funny really, Blade had known immediately whereas it had taken me much longer to realize how strong the ties between us were and would become. Once he had asked me if I would marry him (his religion allowing for multiple wives) and leave the Organization to bear his children. I thought of all the times he'd compared me to the falcons his family used to hunt with when he was a boy, saying that I was small, extremely beautiful, lethally designed and trained for killing. He looked sad but not surprised when I answered, "Can a falcon become a dove?"

I closed my eyes and tried to pretend he was holding me, kissing and biting me, but images of Paul kept intruding. Finished my drink and made another. Kept seeing the look on Paul's face when he thought he would die. The grey color of his skin and his screams as they carried him down the mountain. The sawed-off karabiner. Suddenly I felt trapped in the house—my retreat began to feel more like a prison cell, holding me for the killer. I had to get out. I guess I panicked, but anyway, I got out of there fast and drove to the mountains.

I could feel the tension winding up. Coiling tighter and tighter. The tires shrieked as I yanked the Corvette around a curve. I was driving far too fast.

Slowed down but a moment later the speedometer had crept back up and was hovering at 90. Much too fast at night on these roads. Suddenly I didn't care—to hell with it. The tension was fighting for an outlet and there was one just under my foot. I put it down flat on the floor and found myself grinning into the night as I fought the high-spirited car. At least it was tangible. A car parked by the side of the road was gone almost before it registered. I didn't dare take my eyes off the road long enough to read the speedometer, but the engine was howling like a banshee.

I'd only had a couple days break for the past three months and I'd just been operational for seven weeks straight. Our Africa operator and most of his people had been killed—I sent back what had been left of them for me to find. I finally avenged them but now I badly needed a long spell in a safe place. Long days and weeks to rest and eat, things I seemed to have hardly done for months. To sleep deeply and unwind. To laugh again. To be safe, just for a while. And now I couldn't. Safety was a lie until I neutralized whoever had broken my cover. Even my house wasn't safe now. Nowhere outside of Headquarters was. And I knew I was letting the tension overwhelm me. So I pushed the Corvette as hard as I could and some of the tension spent itself with each curve. And I laughed.

The car flew up into the mountains and the curves got tighter and the drop-offs deeper, and I laughed and laughed and couldn't stop. Somehow I made the final turn to the climbing hut and got the car stopped inches from the abyss beyond. I stopped laughing and sat there until it occurred to me to get out. I remember virtually nothing about that climb. I know I put my rock boots on because I had them on later.

All I remember really is thinking over and over, "If I survive tonight maybe whoever has found me won't kill me. Maybe I'll get them first." Like one of the nursery rhymes my father used to insist my mother read to me even though her English was very poor and she could hardly understand the poems she read from our tattered copy of Milne's *When We Were Very Young*. The one about the cracks in the sidewalk and the bears. If you didn't step on the cracks, the bears wouldn't get you. I hated that poem. It used to give me nightmares as a child. No matter that my mother pronounced "bears" as "beers," there was a picture of them and I knew they were there and waiting for me. Now the bears were real. They'd gotten me once. I still have the scars.

I watched first the false dawn and then the real one from a rock aerie high above the snowline. Numb from the intense cold and numb from fears and memories. Only after the last of the night's shadows had slunk away, did I start the long climb down.

Chapter Two

COMPUTED DEATH

I PACKED as soon as I got back. It was 11:00 A.M. already and I had to be at the Boss's at 12:00. "Get a good night's rest," he'd said! He'd shit little blue kittens if he knew how I'd spent the night. Oh well, I'd sleep on the plane. I grabbed a much-needed hot shower and wolfed down a couple of tuna sandwiches.

Packing took the rest of that hour. I wasn't just packing for a job, which often means only a change of clothes and my toothbrush—I was packing for a typical visit to Belize. Evening clothes to cover any occasion from the Disco to cocktails at the British High Commissioner's house, bikini, hiking clothes, daytime wear for town and old clothes to work in on the farm. I crammed everything into one suitcase and broke a strap trying to get it shut properly.

Took a guy line off my tent and strapped the case shut with that. Made a mental note to buy some gifts for my niece and the rest of the family on my way to the airport. Threw my bag in the car—five minutes to make a ten minute trip—and got caught by the first traffic light. Made the office only a couple minutes late.

The Boss and I went down to consult Lucy, the computer that broods in our basement. I do have to grant that she knows an incredible amount about the political situation in any given country and about terrorist organizations I've never even heard of. I still don't trust her.

She gives the odds on the chances of success of a job based on everything she knows about the country the job will be in, what outside groups might be involved, and what she knows about the operator in charge both from past jobs and from evaluations from the various trainers, doctors, etc., in Headquarters. If the odds are 70-30 or more in favor, the Boss says "go." Sometimes he says "go" anyway, even if the odds are very poor, but only if he has absolutely no choice. Personally, I'd rather not be told by a lump of wires and micro-chips what my chances of dying on a job are. Someday I'm going to pour a cup of hot coffee into Lucy's internal workings and hope it shorts out something irreplaceable.

Lucy's figures are supposed to remain between the Boss and the operator concerned, in this case me, but somehow everyone knows when they're less than 70-30 and the job is going ahead anyway. You know as soon as you walk into Headquarters when someone has gone out on a bad one.

The time of reckoning had arrived. I told myself that Lucy knew more about Belize and me than I do. Not that there should be any problem on this one, it was comparatively a very simple job.

The printout read 50-50. I was shocked. She *must* finally have made a mistake! I glared at the mousy little technician who was ministering to Lucy.

"Are you sure you programmed her correctly?"

"Yes. Of course I did." He tried to look indignant but mostly looked nervous.

"Well, ask her again. This can't be right."

Then the Boss said, "I'm sorry Tessa, but I'm afraid it's correct. I decided to run it through yesterday after you left. I thought perhaps you were right about the additional complications of your being known in Belize outweighing the advantage of your personal knowledge of the country. So, I ran it through for you and two other operators. You were right. Both theirs came out 80-20. You've got yours in your hand.''

''Why didn't you just tell me instead of going through this farce then?'' I felt a total fool for some reason and could cheerfully have chopped Lucy up for scrap iron.

''You wouldn't have believed me.''

True. I wouldn't have! Surely my being known there couldn't make *that* much difference. Some yes, but there had to be something wrong somewhere.

''You can unpack your bags and . . .''

Then I knew what was wrong with Lucy's odds. ''Wait! I don't think she's been asked the right questions.'' The technician did look indignant this time. ''Ask her two questions for me. 'What are my chances of completing the job successfully?' Just that, not including my getting back, and 'What are my chances of personal survival now that my cover has been broken even if I don't do this job?' '' Eyebrows skyrocketed and nobody would meet my eye. Finally the tech said he would need to give her a time frame for the second question, and I made it two weeks, since that was what my normal trips to Belize were.

We waited in silence while Lucy chewed that over. She'd never been asked that way before and it took her longer. Somehow that made her seem more ''human.'' The Boss read the first printout and handed it to me. Job success probability 89-11 in favor. A moment later we were given: Life expectancy of operator during following two-week period 50-50.

''Not much point in unpacking I don't think.''

For once the Boss had nothing to say. We went back up to his office. His wheelchair needed oiling, it squeaked, but I didn't mention it. We talked over details. Our files hadn't yielded any information about my suspect. However, when the Boss decided to have him tailed, he vanished as suddenly as he'd appeared in the first place. Finally, the Boss dismissed me with his usual "Don't let anyone shoot you," and I headed for the armory to collect the gear I'd be taking with me.

Bobby materialized from the far side of the training area with a grenade and a frown. "Fuck'n thing didn't go off. Now I gotta find out why—probably blow up on me. Don't trust these bloody things, worse'n a bloody woman."

"Quit bitching, you like grenades. Set it down *gently* and come sign out my junk. I'll miss my plane if you blow yourself up and I have to go find somebody else to sign me out. You can blow yourself up later."

Bobby grinned, "Friendly bitch, arn't'cha! Okay."

We got out Beauty and Bobby stroked her affectionately before handing her over. She's my personal rifle but I keep her, like the rest of my weapons except my knife, at the armory when I'm not on a job.

Beauty is a gift from Bobby. As head of Training, Bobby hasn't been operational since he left the SAS. On rare occasions though he comes along on a job as an observer to see how well some invention of his acts in the field. Three years ago he came with me on one. He wanted to try out a new variety of explosive he'd come across and I knew I had a bridge that needed blowing. There shouldn't have been a terrorist within five miles for another two hours. . . . As Bobby showed at the river bank the whole place opened up. Never did know if it was a deliberate ambush or just our bad luck, but, whatever, there were about 20 of them. Bobby dived under the bridge abutment for cover but was pinned down. It wasn't going to take long for someone to work around and pitch a grenade under there with him. The only other person with us was the radio man. He'd had only the most basic weapons course and couldn't hit the broad side of a barn.

I left him with orders to get base camp on the horn fast and tell them to get us out *pronto* or they might as well not bother. And to empty his gun in the general direction of anyone trying to approach that bridge. Unless it was me.

I waded the river farther down, out of sight, went up the opposite bank and crossed back beyond the men who'd ambushed us. They hadn't realized there was anyone besides Bobby and the radio man yet. I circled in behind them and higher up the hillside. Found a perfect vantage point. Spent the next hour picking off anyone who moved toward that bridge or tried to cross the road toward the radio man's position. Two tried to flank my position but they never had a prayer of bringing it off. I'd accounted for nine before our people arrived with an armored car, enough fire-power to take out a regiment, and a flame thrower that nearly fried the radio man. Damn fool was so glad to see help that he ran out to them before they were finished mopping up. The guy on the flame thrower just saw a man running at them out of the corner of his eye and swung around. He nearly couldn't stop in time. Those things are hardly precision weapons. Radio man wasn't hurt but he had some laundry to do when he got back. Bobby and I waited till things stopped flying before we came out.

Bobby went back to Headquarters, but another job came up for me the moment we finished that one and I didn't see Bobby again for nearly a month. When I got back and went down to the range, he came over and, after greeting me, handed me a rifle to try out. It was like no rifle I'd ever seen before. When I asked he told me it was a "Crazy Bobby Special." He'd used the principle of the Armalite AR7. Then he'd taken a Mannlicher barrel and action, and threaded it to a custom-made stock modeled after an AR7 stock but a bit bigger. The AR7 is an ideal jungle weapon since it can be taken apart and the separate components fit into the stock, which makes it essentially waterproof and impossible to damage. After swimming a river, you can reassemble it on the other side and be ready to shoot in less than a minute. However, it uses only a .22 bullet which is too lightweight for long-range accuracy and has very little stopping power. Hence the 7.62 Mannlicher barrel and action. Mannlicher is about the best long-range rifle there is, but, of course, can't be taken apart and folded up in its stock. So, Bobby had created an AR7 that would take 7.62 ammo.

And he'd put Aimpoint sights on it. Aimpoint uses an illuminated aiming mark. Since these can be difficult to see against some backgrounds in bright light conditions, Aimpoint has added twin polaroid filters which can be adjusted and even removed entirely for night shooting. The result is an incredibly accurate sight that is easy to use under varying light and target contrast conditions thanks to the combination of brilliance and contrast controls. The only possible drawback to it for my use is that it uses a battery with a 500-hour life. If it should fail for some reason the sight is useless. Trust Bobby, he'd added a compartment for a spare battery.

With Spitzer-type ammo it'd be accurate up to a third of a mile, yet you could carry it in a shoulder bag or drag it through mud or water without damaging it. As the implications sank in, I stared at it in awe. An assassin's dream come true. Bobby handed me a box of ammo and told me to go try her out. She was short barrelled and amazingly light and fitted like she'd been waiting for me. Her trigger was the lightest I'd ever come across on a semi-automatic—you don't really pull the trigger, you just think about it and she fires. She wasn't beautiful, her finish was an odd mottled gray and her lines were too short for classical beauty. She was the ultimate assassin's weapon, and it was love at first sight.

I still remember saying, "God, she's a beauty!," and not quite believing my ears when Bobby said, "Right. Beauty she is. What are you handing her back for? She's yours—if you want her."

"Want her??? *Mine?* Bu—You mean that?"

"Don't think much of me, huh? Don't think my life's worth a bloody gun do ya?"

So, that's Beauty. Bobby's never made another one like her, says it would be sacrilege to copy her. He has never shot her since he gave her to me. He'll cradle her lovingly and occasionally sights down her but he never fires her. I asked him once if he'd like to have a go. Could see he was severely tempted but he handed her back. "You don't fuck a friend's wife. You can admire, you maybe even dream about her, but you don't fuck her."

I patted Beauty for luck, remembering. Bobby punched my arm—he'd been remembering too. "Right, now what else you want?"

"That's it for this time 'cept for my clothes and the bag."

Bobby glared, "Don't be daft, Tessa! I've taught you better than that. You don't go out for a piss on a job relying on just a gun!"

"Beauty's hardly 'just a gun.' And I'll have my knife, always do. It's straight-forward this time—no need for a lot of junk."

"Straight-forward huh? Then how come Lucy said 'No' and the Boss is sending you out anyway? Think you better take a bit more 'junk' with you. At least a garrotte and some plastic, maybe coupla grenades."

"How the hell do you know what Lucy said? Supposedly that stops between the Boss and me, and the grapevine has hardly had time to get to work on it!"

Bobby picked his nose and wiped his finger on his pants before deciding to tell me he'd buttonholed Lucy's tech in the coffee room. "Didn't like what I heard. I know you're not free to tell me what's up and I've never asked you about a job before, but . . .

aw shit! You're go'n anyway, so go on—GO!''

I decided I'd rather not know how Bobby'd persuaded the poor tech, so I inspected my kit until Bobby had his opinions under control, then accepted some plastic, detonators, etc., and a garrotte. Loaded my bag and left, feeling, as always, a bit strange— all dressed up in a good traveling suit, the yellow one that brings out the honey color of my skin, and high heels—and carrying a bag full of death.

Since I was supposed to be on vacation this time, I didn't need to see Maria Teresa about doing an article for me. After all, if a cover is any good, it must be able to stand a good bit of scrutiny, and it would seem a bit peculiar if a ''freelance journalist'' kept appearing all over Latin America waving cameras and press cards— but never had anything published. So, Maria Teresa writes ''my'' stories for me and gets them published in a variety of well-known magazines and newspapers. She is a brilliant writer and I some- times wonder how she can stand to never be able to accept the praise due her, herself. But she has her reasons for being with the Watchdog Organization, the same as the rest of us. Her entire family was killed after her father, a history professor, spoke out against the brutality of the right-wing generals in the Guatemalan army. She is alive only because she was finishing her last year at Harvard studying journalism at the time. She immediately dropped out and joined the World Council for Human Rights. Soon after, she was passed on to the Watchdog Organization. She writes cover articles for a number of our people besides me, does an incredible amount of research and never sleeps as far as I can tell. Her intensity always makes me uncomfortable so I was glad to give her office a miss this time.

I stopped around by Maintenance and asked Jimmy to run me out to the airport. He grinned and told his assistant to mind the shop. Jimmy is our chief mechanic and a genius. He can fix absolutely anything. He's also a stereo buff and the guy responsible for my sound system. Whenever I need someone to drop me off or collect me from the airport I ask him. I don't like leaving my car at the airport when I'm gone. Someday somebody might leave a little present under the hood for me. I know it's clean if it's been at Headquarters. Jimmy's always glad of an excuse to get out for a bit and he loves my car. It's a 1965 Corvette, white with a red leather interior. I like old sports cars. Drove it into the shop the day I bought it and couldn't get it back from Jimmy for nearly a week! He left his assistants to cope with all the Organization's work and worked 'round the clock on the 'Vette. It looked okay when I bought it. I damn near didn't recognize it when he finally let me have it back. It was absolutely gorgeous. He'd repainted it for a start—think he went over it bolt by bolt. When he finished it, it was in more than mint condition, and he's kept it like that ever since. Strips it down completely everytime I leave it for an oil change—that's the only problem, I can never get it back in less than two days. Jimmy's played with the engine as well. It'll do 140 without a whimper.

I stopped at a shopping center to get gifts for my family in Belize. Ken and his wife and the twins were easy, but Gayle is almost impossible to shop for. Never know what my niece is going to be "into" from one trip to the next. Eight-year-old girls change their minds as often as their clothes. I usually cope by taking one "safe" gift with me, then sending her something appropriate to her latest interest when I get back. Last time it was Elvis Presley. Time before it was medieval tapestries. God only knew what it would be this time! Finally chose a necklace—she likes jewelry almost as much as I do.

The airport was half-empty as I checked through. My carry-on bag, another of Bobby's creations, has a false bottom that is superbly concealed and lined with various layers meant to confuse airport scanners. So far it's never failed. As always, I touched wood and went through with no fuss. The girl smiled a plastic smile as she handed back my bag. I wondered how she'd react if she knew she'd just handed me my gun, various explosives and a dagger.

It's an antique dagger, Spanish, Toledo steel with a carved ebony hilt. Bobby claims there are better knives around, but it fits my hand and I refuse to trade it. It used to hang on the wall in the study of a wealthy Spanish industrialist whose family was kidnapped and held for ransom. He never knew I was the one who got them back alive, thought I was strictly liaison, but he appreciated what he did know. I'd admired the dagger greatly from the moment I saw it, so, with typical Spanish courtesy but mixed feelings because I was a woman, he gave it to me. Along with enough Chanel No. 5 to last two lifetimes.

I went into the boarding lounge and found an empty seat. I glanced out the window and saw heavy clouds pouring down from the mountains—couldn't see the mountains at all. An hour later the day's flights were cancelled. Can't fly when you can barely see your hand in front of your face, not even with modern technology, not with the mountains that close.

I finally got to a telephone and had Jimmy come get me. Went back to Headquarters. Should've gone home to bed, but I knew I wouldn't sleep, just brood. And the paperwork never stopped flowing into my office, no matter how long I was gone. I sighed and resigned myself to tackling some of it. I walked in and couldn't even see my desk, just papers. A disgusting number had red flags on them. I stalled as long as possible by making a cup of coffee and switching on the computer console, etc. Half an hour later I had it sorted into piles. An hour later I'd shovelled off about half the piles onto other peoples' IN trays. I was still left with a horrendous pile, 90 percent of it red-flagged.

I left it and went over to the computer console. I had to know where my key people were and what they were doing before I could start trying to put out the most urgent fires. Didn't bother to check on Gretchen or Raul, I'd left them holding the fort behind me until the new Africa team was sent over. Raul should be released for leave as soon as possible, but I doubted he'd get any, not with that many red flags on my desk. Still, he'd be okay—he never seemed to want much leave anyway, so I'd be able to use him as soon as he got back. Gretchen was also due leave but I knew she'd refuse it, she liked to save it up and then go disappear off into the hinterlands of Norway with her brothers for a couple of months. She once said something about raw fish and caribou—whatever, the rest of the time she's the best pilot we have. God knows she'd just proved that again, dodging everything from machine-gun fire to stingers in order to fetch me out a couple of times when it got too hot. I shuddered inside, remembering the things she made that damn tinkertoy she calls a helicopter do. Evasive action, she'd said, and smiled serenely while things were blowing up all around us and it seemed to me we were flying on our side, something I don't think helicopters can do. But Gretchen smiled and gently hummed while wrenching the controls, and us, all over hell's half acre until we were safe and she could drop me off to start the hunt all over again.

I hauled myself back to the present and punched at the console. Paco: he and Raul worked together whenever possible—and made an excellent team. They looked like brothers, both short, dark, compact, and fantastically strong, but Raul's Mexican and Paco, Uruguayan. Paco'd been with me at the beginning in South Africa but I'd sent him out as courier with info for the Boss I didn't want to trust to any code, also to help Jacques with the bodies. Console said Paco was in Mexico on bodyguard detail. Due back today. Good.

The Assassin and the Deer

Jacques was actually here at Headquarters so I could lay hands on him right away. Poor guy—he wasn't due leave but needed some. A superb medic and, if need be, field surgeon, but the only member of our Africa's team who'd been left alive for us to find had been long beyond anyone's help. All Jacques could do was give him morphine to ease the last couple of hours. I ordered him to give the poor man an overdose and get it over with, but he refused, tears streaming down his face. Unfortunately, his interpretation of the Hippocratic oath leaves no room for mercy killing unless the patient himself asks for it and will clearly die soon anyway. But you can't ask anything if some bastard has cut out your tongue, and since the same bastard had burned out our man's eyes, he couldn't even ask that way. I sent Jacques outside while I shot him—no morphine in the world could kill that amount of pain without also killing what remained of the man. I wondered if Jacques had forgiven me yet. Or ever would. Yes, in time, if he lived long enough. In time, he would do it himself, when he'd seen enough agony that he couldn't cure. Okay, one medic available and more or less functional. Not much compared to the stack on my desk.

That took care of the key people I'd taken with me, now, who else was around? Mmm. Better check on Maria and José. Oh shit! Some idiot had loaned them to Intelligence and they were back in Rio, where I'd first found them. Damn damn damn. Their files were heavily flagged so that NO ONE could assign them without my authority—but some idiot had anyway, and they'd gone although they knew they shouldn't, because they'd have been bored hanging around here. But turning them loose is a bit like pulling the pins on a couple of hand grenades and tossing them out of a plane with no idea where they'll land. Those two kids are absolutely brilliant—and absolutely without any morals whatsoever. To hell with it, Intelligence could pay for all they'd steal and whoever had suffered from their ideas of fun.

That left Tenzing. Computer said he was here doing a refresher course. Tenzing needs a refresher course like he needs a hole in the head. Good. I'd put him in charge of whatever was worst in that pile. Very young but more sense than most people, and being Gurkha, he can pass as Latin American easily.

Another hour and I'd done all I could and left written instructions for whoever the Boss put in my office until I came back. If I came back. I badly needed a good secretary or assistant or whatever. But if someone is good enough to understand the actualities of Wet Work and the strains it imposes on its personnel, chances are good that person is usable in the field, and we are desperately short of good field people. An office type who could understand why Maria and José should NEVER be let loose untended, or why Raul and Paco together were more than twice either of them alone— that's a rare creature. Europe had a good secretary; so does Asia; North America has given up and does its own, like me; Africa had a new one it was hopeful about, but that was the body they'd left tied over an anthill. . . . God! I've gotta stop seeing it all again. Somehow I've gotta wipe out the last seven weeks like they never existed.

No way in this bloody office though—the empty walls acted like screens for the scenes my mind kept replaying. I fled to the training center and Bobby.

Didn't see him on the main floor so tried the armory. Forgot he doesn't allow anyone else in there besides me, at least not without an invitation. He turned around with a ferocious glare, then looked half-disgusted, half pleased.

"What's this then, a fuckin' ghost or summat?? Tessa left here hours ago!"

"Just wanted another cuppa coffee's all. In case you haven't noticed, there's a storm outside that's getting worse by the minute.

Started out a few hours ago with one solid bank of fog, so they cancelled all flights.''

"Oh yeah? War managed to get in, what 'e do, walk?''

"War's back? Must've come on an early flight and brought the storm with him.''

"Umm. Betcha 'e walked! Bastard probly could 'n all—'e's around here somewhere if you wanna go dance wi' 'im.''

"Maybe later. I don't feel very bouncy at the moment.''

"Yeah, you look like shit too.''

"THANKS, bloody pommy.''

"Tha's bleed'n pommy, if you must insult me, at least get it right. A workout'll do ya good. Go get out a those wiggle-ass clothes and ina someth'n more comfortable-like. . . .''

I faked a kick at his head and went off to change, leaving him laughing behind me. Bobby always calls my good clothes "wiggle-ass clothes'' and I'll kill him for it some day. And I should never have said that my old leotard was the most comfortable thing I owned—I'll never, ever live that down. Gotta get a new one, one a these days, it's positively gray with age. The ragged holes where I cut off the sleeves don't improve its looks either. But dammit it is comfortable.

Bobby wandered out with me when I went to look for War. We finally found him showing off for some new recruits who looked suitably impressed. I always forget that someone can really be that big. Bobby couldn't resist needling him and told the recruits, "Now you'll see a real expert.'' They looked around to see what giant he meant and assumed he was kidding when he gestured to me. War ignored him and swept me up in a bear hug that nearly broke my spine before dropping me and breaking into a Zulu war dance. I was more than a bit surprised, I mean, we get on pretty well, but that's not his normal welcome. Then he came to a jarring stop in front of me and stated something in an African dialect I didn't know before grinning from ear to ear and announced, "I've got Africa! I'm going HOME!! I'm going to be the BOSS man! A little bird told me you did it!"

"Hey! Hold on. I might've said something or I might not have, but you wouldn't be promoted Africa section head unless you were the best choice. Anyhow, congratulations! I'm delighted to hear it." I grinned at War and thought, for the umpteenth time, how incongruous his clipped British accent was coming from his huge, blue-black frame.

"Well, that little bird told me you stuck your neck way out, even *argued* with the Boss. It told me that is the only reason I got the job."

Shit. Who in hell had overheard us? "War, *nobody* argues with the Boss!" Then I had to say it but I didn't know how. Finally asked, "Have you read the report I made when I got in?"

The grin vanished. "Yes, my dear. I did. I just wish I'd been the one to revenge our people."

"No. Better this way. You'll be a new, unknown face. Too many people saw me. I could never organize our Africa end of things even if I had the knowledge and wanted to leave my sector."

"Maybe you're right, but it doesn't feel right. You've just spent seven weeks on the far side of Hell so I can go in with everything all tidy and ready to start over. It's not fair to you."

The far side of Hell. Jesus, he was so right. Those were the first words that made any sense out of the last seven weeks. I felt something give inside myself and heard myself stuttering, except that I never stutter, "I . . . I . . . I didn't for you, I did for . . . for . . . for them. For us . . . for all of us. You . . . you should . . . know. Every s-s-single person . . . here . . . here when . . . the message came. . . . Every single person . . . even office . . . office people . . . volunteered."

Bobby was shaking me and War scooped me up and carried me back to the armory. The trainees trailed after us asking questions until Bobby turned on them. Then War was holding me on his lap, murmuring soothing nonsense words, like you do to hurt children, and Bobby was forcing straight rum down my throat and I shook and shook like I had the worst case of malaria in history.

Finally, I pulled myself together to sit without help. Bobby looked at War and asked, "That bad??"

War stared at him for a long moment and somehow, War-the-British gentleman and War-the-African warrior were gone, and a bitter heartsick stranger was left who said simply, "My people are capable of doing things that no animal would lower itself to do. Yes, it was that bad." The silence hung between us. War spoke again, so low we could barely hear him as he said, "I read the report and then I threw up."

Bobby looked at me with a look that shouted 'You gotta *do* somethin'!,' and I began speaking without knowing what I was going to say, only that I had to reach War somehow.

"Quit it, big man. Cut the drama. Yes, your people can be horrendously cruel, but they sure as shit don't have any monopoly on it. I just wish they did. Then we could bomb Africa off the face of the earth and everybody else'd live happily ever after. . . . Trouble is, there's never been anyone crueler than the Spaniards who ran the Inquisition. Unless it's the Chinese, on and off, ever since civilization got started. Or the Aztecs who sacrificed children as well as warriors, by the thousands, till their streets were flooded with blood to appease their gods. The Sioux and Apache had a few tricks up their sleeves too, most of them very similar to those your people use. And if you say that's past history and everyone else has grown up except you poor ignorant savages down in blackest Africa, try telling that to the survivors of the German concentration camps. Or the families of those who've 'disappeared' all over

Latin America. Or the victims of the child porn and snuff films in
the USA and Europe for God's sake!!! Shit, man, I can't even
think of a single torture your precious blacks have a monopoly
on!''

War looked at me like he'd never seen me before in his life.
Then he started to laugh and he laughed until he cried, and then he
laughed some more. I felt totally drained—first coming apart at
the seams—then it had been one hell of a gamble, and I began to
realize how much that big mountain of meat matters in my world
when I knew I might just have made him hate me. But I had to do
something to bring his private agony into perspective, even if it
meant losing his friendship.

Bobby passed the bottle around and then told us to go 'dance'
and impress his trainees. War and I grinned. ''Will he run us over
again do you think?''

''Naw, he's gett'n older, probably can't push that much weight
now.''

We both ducked as Bobby swung the rum bottle at us.

''You wanna bet?? Just try play'n bloody damn fools 'n see
what hits you *this* time!''

War rubbed his head and grimaced—he'd gotten a concussion
out of our first encounter—and I rubbed imaginary ribs and let my
arm dangle—I'd wound up with two busted ribs and a dislocated
shoulder. But neither of us would have been alive if Bobby hadn't
somehow shoved a loaded forklift weighing around a ton and a
half into us seconds before we killed each other. He'd set us up in
competition and War was new and couldn't believe a woman could
beat him at fighting skills. He blew a fuse when we got to hand-to-
hand combat and was a split second from breaking my neck, so I
broke all training rules and drew my hand back to drive my fingers
through his eye, into his brain. But the forklift hit us square on just
in time. After War came to, he half-carried me into the armory and

appropriated Bobby's bottle which we shared until the medics arrived. We've mutually respected each other ever since, but never really fight. We go through all the moves but it's different—more like a ballet of perfect timing. We're too evenly matched and, I think, both afraid of unleashing ourselves again. So Bobby says we dance. Whatever it is, it's magic, like the best of dancing and the best of fighting at once, but without the fear and rage.

We played for an hour, karate kicks and strikes, judo throws and all the standard repertoire, then Bobby threw a glass half-full of rum to War, who plucked it out of the air without spilling a drop while spinning away from a kick. As his spin returned him to me, the glass left his hand aimed at my face at a ferocious speed. I barely caught it. Juggled it from hand to hand while dodging round his attempts to close with me, then threw it at his crotch and kicked at his face. He caught the glass, still without spilling a drop, but fumbled and let my foot touch his temple. I'd have killed him if I hadn't deflected my kick. War handed the glass back to Bobby and bowed to me. I bowed in return as Bobby told the stunned trainees, "See? Told ya she was better!"

A voice spoke from behind us, a voice that flowed through me like warm honey, saying, "He is merely a WOG and therefore of no importance."

"NO IMPORTANCE! No importance my left nut! I'll show you who's of no importance." War's roar was of a truly impressive volume. "Anyway, WOG is short for Worthy *Oriental* Gentleman—you're the only WOG around here, not me!"

My Afghani rebel pursed his lips thoughtfully. "My, my, the Nigras are getting educated these days, how very surprising. I beg your pardon War, I was unaware that you could read. I believed crude spears to be more your, um, style." (Blade knew as well as I did that War held two degrees from Cambridge and one from the University of London.)

War would've continued the discussion except he was laughing too hard, and Blade couldn't since I was wrapped around him, giving him a very thorough "hello." Bobby was rolling in the aisles but the trainees looked like they were expecting bloodshed. Then one of those sudden silences fell which left one lone voice shouting to his companions, "If she's the black heavy's friend, then how come she's kissing some guy who just insulted him?"

War and I started laughing again—only Bobby knew how badly we needed to laugh that day. (Or so I thought at the time, later I found out Blade knew too. Knowing how seldom Blade jokes, I guessed then that that was the reason he started it all in the first place.) But that was later. Now Bobby shooed us all out bitching that he couldn't be expected to teach with us doing a comedy routine in the middle of his training center.

War excused himself, grinning from ear to ear, a rather considerable distance. He pounded Blade on the shoulder and then turned to me and held out his hand. When I put mine into it, mine disappeared completely. I was glad I was on his side. "Thank you, my dear." He started to say something else but glanced at Blade and walked off instead.

Blade and I were walking out of the training center when he said, "I've never seen you . . . in motion before."

I couldn't help a giggle.

"You must've been sleeping a lot then when you seemed to be pretty awake!"

"Oh, no, I did not mean motion in that sense, I should have said I never saw you train before. I had not realized such a large man could be so very fast. Nor did I realize such a small woman could be even faster!!" His obvious admiration made me feel like someone had just put a crown on my head.

"I was just teasing you, I knew what you meant."

"English is a very complex language. Every time I think I

have finally learned it correctly, then you make jokes with me because I have used a word incorrectly—again. Yet you are an ignorant half-breed infidel who cannot even say my name without calling me 'an unclean pig in Allah's garden!' You are a most cruel and unfair barbarian!''

Unfortunately, he was right—I do pronounce his name so it comes out meaning a pig in Allah's garden. His proper name should translate as Shining Blade of Allah. He got tired of hearing his name butchered so suggested we just call him Blade, the name he'd gone by for five years in England, where he took advanced training in economics and intelligence techniques.

I tried to look suitably abashed but failed completely. He took my hand and angled me out toward the parking lot. ''Shall we go to Papacito's? It is a little early for dinner but we could always have some wine first.''

''What, a good Moslem like yourself suggesting *alcoholic* beverages?''

''I am not a good Moslem, I am a very bad Moslem, and I would settle for almost anything as long as it is an alcoholic beverage!''

''Right, Papacito here we come. Your car or mine?''

''Mine. You look tired. Also you know I feel silly being driven by a woman.''

Blade can be astoundingly chauvinistic at times, he truly does feel silly if I drive. I watched his dark hawk features, their cruelty relieved only by his eyes, huge liquid black bedroom eyes with eyelashes most women would kill for. But as we drove his eyes went bleak and flat. I didn't know what was wrong but I moved over next to him and stroked the back of his neck. After a moment he relaxed and the bleak look receded. We didn't speak until the storm ushered us into Papacito's.

Papacito is a small round man who has seen some of the worst the world can offer, and suffered through the loss of one after another of his family until he had only one blood relation, a second cousin, left. He is the kindest man I know. He rushed up, hugging and patting us both, ushering us to a private table in the back, calling for coffee for three then changing that to wine, exclaiming about the weather and generally fussing over us as if we were a combination of family and royalty. Sometimes he sits with us, this time he knew we wanted to be alone, so he left after depositing an assortment of bottles of our favorite drinks and glasses on a cart next to our table. We said we'd order later, but he sent over two bowls of some sort of spicy soup which went down beautifully.

We asked him to choose our meal, saying only that we were hungry (I'd never had lunch and Blade had only had the early morning "breakfast" they'd pushed at him on his flight in. Like War, he arrived just before I got to the airport, while the weather was still fairly clear.)

It was good to sit across from Blade while the wind howled outside and the rain tried to creep under the shutters. We'd finished off a good bit of liquor by the time Papacito came beaming out of the kitchen, bearing a huge tray that smelled like heaven. Leisurely, we finished the enormous platter of slivers of lamb and veal, fresh vegetables and tiny pastry-covered bits and pieces, all crisped a piece at a time in the pot of simmering oil and burgundy set over a brazier in the center of the table.

The remnants were whisked away and a truly glorious Peking duckling, which Papacito carved exquisitely, was set before us along with numerous bowls of rice, lightly steamed bamboo shoots and water chestnuts, plums simmered in brandy and a dozen more bowls of unidentifiable delicacies. Blade and I were stunned— Papacito had never served us anything Oriental before. We gaped like idiots.

Papacito asked anxiously if that would be all right?

We assured him it would be *more* than all right, and we would move in permanently if he produced food like this every day! He'd gotten bored with his (excellent) repertoire of Latin American and European food, so had taught himself the arts of Oriental cooking. This was the first time he'd tried the results on customers. He was thrilled that we were so obviously impressed and we guaranteed to spread the word.

Eventually, we staggered out into the storm again and made it to my place. We collapsed on the sofa and groaned until Blade summoned up the energy to make us a couple of Irish coffees to wash down into any tiny cracks that remained.

Twenty minutes later I got up, poured Blade a double brandy, and retreated to my bathroom. First I washed all the grime and sweat off. Then I oiled every inch of my body with my own mix of coconut oil, honey and my favorite musky perfume. What to wear . . . um . . . skip the nighties and all the kinky bits. Just jewelry tonight. The ruby choker, matching ring, earrings and ankle bracelet . . . what else? Ah, that gorgeous ruby and gold creation Blade had indulged me with, solid heavy bands of gold that wrapped around my hips and curved down to join in a vee of gold mesh and rubies, smaller rubies at the top of the triangle, larger ones below and ending in a single gorgeous stone that dangled right at the tip of my own triangle. Checked the mirror. Shook my hair loose to fall down over my hips. Yes, that would do. The oil, highlighted by the gold and rubies made me look like a golden bronze statue. Pure sexual female animal looked back at me from the mirror. Never mind the shaky nerves, the pounding veins in my wrists and hands, now I was not Tessa, not an assassin, I was *woman*. Let women's lib spin in its grave, I was determined to listen to far older rhythms tonight, rhythms that were old when the earth was born.

Blade was still drinking. He was also throwing my throwing

knives at the kitchen door, just completing the outline of a bear as I walked past him to the tape deck. Put on a Balinese tape and began to dance. One thing I can do besides kill is dance. Despite the climbing and the unarmed combat lessons, I've kept my hands and feet supple enough through yoga to do the formal moves of the Balinese classics. And what looks stiff and slow to western eyes when the dancers are wearing heavy costumes, becomes pure erotica performed naked except for a few pieces of jewelry, when each angled leg is outlined against the few soft lights I'd left on, when the coils of pubic hair show each time you turn in profile or bend a leg. Blade stopped throwing knives.

The tape ended and I put on a West African drum tape, a snake dance one. I had no snake but I wove one out of the air, passing my imaginary snake around and over my body, between my legs, across my belly, up flicking first one breast, then the other. My hips kept the rhythm, my feet never moved, my hands played the snake and my face pantomimed sex, birth, death, rebirth and sex. Blade had a hard on I could see from across the room.

When I finished I shone with sweat as well as oil and headed for the kitchen to make a very cold vodka martini. Blade followed me in and nuzzled me but I could feel his heart wasn't really in it. I sat on the sink, wrapped my legs around his waist and held him silently.

He pushed me away and stared at me. I waited. We'd not yet spoken about anything that had happened since I left. We would, but not tonight. So I didn't know he'd read my report, knew how I'd spent the last seven weeks. I only knew something was very wrong.

He started to speak twice, then abruptly asked, "Do you trust anyone?"

"I trust Bobby. I trust the Boss. And I trust you."

"Prove it."

"How do you want me to?"

Blade pushed me away, still staring at me. "The knives."

I asked him what he meant.

"Stand against the door while I throw the knives."

I did a quick assessment—Blade had had a hell of a lot to drink and was weaving slightly as he stood. However, I'd never seen him miss with one of those knives. Besides, I could always deflect them if I had to, though he obviously didn't know that. I saw in his eyes that I'd lose him if I didn't. I might anyway, I didn't know what the hell was going on, but no way would I risk losing him.

I walked over to the door in answer.

"Kali, goddess of death, do you trust me or do you not care?"

Kali??

"Here, I forgot to give you this. Here, take your alter ego."

He was holding out something green. I reached out and he set a tiny jade figurine in my hand. Kali. Dancing on a pile of skulls, each hand holding a different weapon, a serene, infinitely cruel smile on her face. Kali, the Hindu goddess of death. Kali, whose followers killed for her with squares of black silk, garrotting their chosen victims for the glory of their bloodthirsty goddess. I stared at the little figurine. Her features were mine—the same high cheek bones, the same eyes. Her figure was mine, the same full round breasts, the tiny waist flaring into ripe hips, a short-coupled, provocative body. I felt like throwing up. Then something snapped.

I'd reached for Blade to erase the horror and fear, he handed me Kali and wanted to throw knives at me. Okay. Kali he wants, Kali he fucking well gets. My hands shook when I set the evil little goddess down on my bookcase—but they didn't shake when I assumed her pose in front of the door. Well, assumed it as well as a two-armed being could assume a pose requiring four arms.

Blade turned around, a knife in each hand, and froze. I pulled my lips into a facsimile of her smile and waited, standing, one leg bent slightly, the other at right angles, touching my knee, foot bent out and down. One arm curved above my head, fingers bent back and up, the other curved down beside my waist. I stepped out of the pose a split second, grabbed a silk runner off the bookcase and twisted my hair up in it in a facsimile of Kali's headdress, and resumed my stance—a bloody strenuous and uncomfortable one I might add. But I was beyond tiredness or sore muscles or any human need. Blade wanted Kali; I'd give him Kali, in spades.

He wavered, something very akin to fear in his eyes.

"The knives. Show me Kali on the door."

He shook himself slightly and began to throw. Retrieve and throw. He outlined me perfectly, each knife a quarter of an inch from my skin.

He started to put them away. I spoke. "There are more in the side drawer, all equally well-balanced."

He looked puzzled but got them.

"Now, kill Kali if you can."

He stared at me. "What do you mean, 'kill Kali'?"

"Throw your puny little knives AT me, not beside me."

"NO!!"

I was out of my skull, I admit, but I'd had too damn much and this charade was sick. If Blade wanted to flirt with death, he'd learn that death could flirt back. And I'd been death, lived with death and fear and horror for too long. War and Bobby and Papacito had purged some of it but Blade had handed it all back with that horrible little jade figurine dancing on the skulls of her victims. Blade had never seen that side of me, only guessed and glamorized from rumors and talk around Headquarters. Well, he could have that side of me too, tonight.

I smiled slowly and stepped away from the door toward him. Slowly I reached up to where the two ornamental kukris hung and took them out of their scabbards. Blade knew as well as I did that you never took the Gurkha knives out without letting them taste blood, your own if no one else's. The large blade in my left, the small dagger in my right, I stepped back against the door and resumed Kali's pose.

The silence stretched. Death moved around the room, invited but blind. Blade's skin went gray and sweaty and his eyes darted around the room. Then he made a visible effort, knelt and addressed a short speech to me / Kali in his native dialect which I couldn't understand. Then threw as he stood up. Good, but I flicked it away with the dagger. Five more times he threw, at my eyes, my heart, my throat, and once a low try for my ankle, the one I was standing on. I nearly lost my balance getting that one. Then the knives lay around me like fallen leaves and I smiled.

"Come, let us end this. Pick up your toys and I will put mine away and I shall meet you with my body alone."

"Tessa, please, no. Tessa!"

"No. You want Kali. Now learn who she is. Learn and never call her again." I gently drew the Gurkha knives over my thighs, leaving thin trails of blood behind, before sheathing them. Then I resumed Kali's pose.

"Throw your toys."

The first knife he threw slowly, giving me as much time as possible. I waited until it was roughly a foot from my midriff, then snap kicked it away.

The second one came faster. Again I kicked it away, using the side of my foot against the handle. Then I began to weave back and forth, dancing as I waited. That was too much for Blade's ego and the next four were meant to kill. Each one spun aside as I hit the junction of blade and hilt with the edges of my hands. God, the hours I've spent learning that from our ancient Korean trainer. Never thought I'd use that knowledge against my lover!

I suddenly realized Blade was kneeling before me, head bowed, exposing his neck to me. A litany of strange symbols, then, "Kali, I have errored. Take my life if it pleases you. Take my life, only go back to your heavenly throne. Take my life and be satisfied. Take no other, for I alone summoned you."

Jesus Christ on a fucking bicycle!! How did we get here? Something still remained to finish this charade, only it wasn't a charade, never had been, I'd been the only one fool enough to think so. And yet I couldn't completely deny what surged in my blood. I left Blade kneeling and stumbled (I'd been standing on one foot for a long time) over to the bookcase. I stared at the little jade figurine. She stared back and I swear she smiled into my eyes, probing for my soul. I turned her around, then systematically, ritualistically Blade would say, I broke off each of her delicate arms and legs before I broke off her head. When it was finished I carried the pieces back to Blade and dropped them in front of him.

"Tessa?"

"Yes."

"Is . . ."

"Kali is gone. I . . . I think I killed her this time. But don't ever call her again. She . . . I . . . there's been . . . there've been so many deaths."

"Yes. Darling, I know. I'm sorry. No, I'm not, I had to know. I've been a fool, I've glamorized something you hate."

"But Kali is always there."

"She doesn't own your soul. I . . . I had to know. May Allah have mercy on my soul, I had to know."

"Why now?"

"I read your debriefing. I have clearance and a good friend was on loan to your African section. I didn't know it was you when I asked for the file, I just wanted to know if my friend was alive."

"No one was alive."

"I know. And I'm glad you killed those responsible, but there were a lot of deaths. Some were worthy of Kali at her worst. There was reason and more. But I had to know if you were still Tessa or if Kali had seduced you.''

''Not before tonight.''

''Allah! Forgive me, forgive me my heart. I could not live without you but I could not live with myself if I loved a woman who wanted only to kill.''

''That's why you offered me . . . Kali . . . your life?''

''Yes.''

''Jesus!'' I stood up and headed for the bathroom, stripping off my jewelry as I went. Ran a tub as hot as I could stand it and sank into it until only my nose and eyes were above water. A few minutes later the door opened and Blade came in carrying two frozen daiquiris. They melted while he scrubbed my back. Then he slid into the bathtub beside me, and into me. A long while later most of the bathwater was on the floor, although we had been very gentle and cautious in our lovemaking. We dried each other off and moved to the bedroom.

The next day I tried to sleep on the plane but the stewardesses kept waking me up to ask if I wanted a drink. Not before lunch, thank you. I finally gave up on sleep and found myself thinking about Bobby instead. He knows me so well—should do, he's taught me nearly everything I know about my job. Improved my shooting and my knife work no end, spent one hell of a lot of hours training me in all forms of unarmed combat—so many ways of killing. As much as anything else, he's taught me that *anything* can be a weapon—a pencil, a book, a spoon—anything. I could almost hear him telling me, ''Don't throw a cup, smash it across the bridge a the bastard's nose. It'll break 'n with a bit a' luck 'e'll get a piece in 'is eye—if you're really lucky, a piece'll go right on inta 'is brain.''

And he'd been the one who made me understand the necessity for the Watchdog Organization—oh, the Boss had explained that societies needed people like us to protect them from the wolves outside the walls, even if they don't want to admit the things which have to be done to protect them. But that was pretty abstract when I'd just had to torture a man for the first time. I knew the information I got had been critical to saving a plane load of hostages, but I was still very upset and considering quitting the Organization. Bobby hauled me down to the armory, waited till I was ready to listen and then just said, "Look, wouldn't it a been a good thing ta have someth'n like the World Council for Human Rights around when Hitler decided to kill off all a the Jews? Well, 'n how long you figger any World Council investigator woulda lasted if 'e'd tried ta investigate the concentration camps—maybe two minutes? So, 'e woulda needed someone like us to ride shotgun for 'im, even if 'e didn' know we was there, right? Ok, now, what would you've done if you was that person 'n you saw a trainload a Jews be'n taken off ta be gassed—would ya kill the guards 'n free 'em iff'n you could or would you say naw, kill'n not nice? 'Course you'da killed the guards. Well, guy you tortured was gonna get 'bout one hundred and forty-seven innocent people who had the bad luck ta pick that one flight killed 'less you stopped him—just your tough luck you had ta hurt 'im ta make 'im tell you 'bout the bomb. So one hundred and forty-seven are alive 'n you're sitti'n 'round feel'n sorry for yourself. Kinda stupid, aintcha?"

He's the only one who understands the risks, what it's like to be hunted—or what it's like when you wish they'd killed you instead. Or who understands the decisions you have to make sometimes, when every decision is wrong and you must choose the least wrong one. The one with the fewest dead bodies afterwards. Decisions that must be made when you're exhausted, mentally and physically both, and made with inadequate information—and which can never be unmade afterwards. Blade understands to a certain extent, but not completely.

Bobby's mind is a bit warped but so would anyone's be whose

best mate was killed in Ireland—by a six-inch nail being driven into his skull, slowly. Or who had two metal kneecaps as a result of having his drilled by the IRA. Bobby spent eighteen months learning to walk again. He was told it was hopeless but he refused to believe the doctors. Drank a bottle of whisky a day—drank till he could stand the pain, then forced his knees to bend with his hands. Screaming with pain till he couldn't stand it any longer. Then the bottle again and he'd repeat the whole process. He finally regained full use of his legs but at an unbelievable cost. He worked for the SAS as a trainer for several more years till he did something that got him kicked out. Don't know what. I've never asked. Don't really know why Bobby and I have become so close, we just have. Even if he did nearly kill me.

It never woulda happened if I'd reacted like he'd been trying to teach me. But I panicked and started struggling and something snapped inside Bobby's head—don't think I've ever been so scared shitless in my adult life as I was then, when I saw the wanting-to-kill in his eyes and knew he didn't even remember who I was. Maybe if I could've spoken, but he had me around the throat and I couldn't speak or breathe or anything and all I knew was the terrible feeling of pressure, bulging my eyes until I thought they'd burst. That, and the look in Bobby's eyes. Then a glimmer of hope as I saw him look almost puzzled and mutter something about ''why aren't you struggling, struggle damn you, fight!'' I realized that somehow, in my horror, I'd stopped fighting and that was confusing him. So I made myself hang limp, letting him kill me, not fighting him, willing him to recognize me.

I blacked out before he dropped me. When I came to he was sitting on the floor, staring at his hands with tears streaming down his cheeks. Then I heard him asking, ''Why'd I kill my Tessa?'' Gagging for air I dragged myself over to him. He didn't see me until I pulled at his knee. Then he just stared at me—I don't think he could believe I was alive, then the horror and guilt flooded his face and he tried to push me away but I wouldn't let go. I knew it had to be made right then or it never could be. I couldn't speak yet so I tried to grin. Must've looked god-awful but he realized it was meant to be a grin. I never saw anybody look so stunned in my life. Then he was hugging me and we were both still on the floor hugging with his tears soaking us both when one of the other trainers came in, gaping like someone was strangling *him*—we never did explain, or ever mention it again. There was no need to. I knew before that Bobby was a man incapable of leaving the world of death; I'm finding it more and more difficult to do so myself. Though I don't enjoy killing—fortunately—I've seen too many people who do, and know killing can be the most addictive drug of all. Damn Blade's Kali shit anyway! Last night still had me spooked. Bloody evil little figurine. I made myself think about Gayle instead. She is my tie to sunlight and laughter and eight-year-old girls who aren't charred corpses but beautifully alive and demanding in their surety that they are the center of the universe. Who knows, maybe they are. Eight-year-old girls and kittens and puppies seem as good reasons as any for the existence of the world.

Gayle is a strangely perceptive child. And she's going to be a raving beauty when she grows up. Where she gets her flaming hair from, nobody's figured out, no one else in the family has red hair. Whatever, that hair and her eyes that are as green as mine—she's going to break some hearts when she gets a bit older. She's no-body's fool either. I like her kid sisters, the terrible twins—well, from a distance anyway—but they've never taken Gayle's place in my affections.

I met her for the first time about six years ago, when I first met my brother. Half-brother really. Shortly after I started work for the Organization and actually had some spare cash for the first time in my life, I hired a firm to trace my father. It took 18 months.

Considering that I'd last seen him 20 years before, no one knew where he'd gone, and most of the people who'd known him were dead or had left West Africa, it was surprising they ever traced him at all. Turned out he'd gone to the United States where he'd married shortly afterwards, apparently just not mentioning the wife and child he'd left behind. His new wife promptly bore him a son. My father died in a car accident a few years later.

After some thinking, I asked the firm to find my half-brother. A few months later they told me he'd left the States and moved to Belize, where his wife was born. I wrote to them. They invited me to visit. Once Ken got over the shock of finding out his father'd had a previous family and deserted them, he and Sarah treated me as if I were his full sister. I had trouble thinking of a young American farmer as my brother, but I had no trouble at all feeling that Gayle was a blood relation. Apparently, when you're two years old, as she was then, accepting a new relative is easy. Anyway, Gayle made me feel like I was family from the first moment we met and she offered me half of the remainder of a well-sucked lollipop. We finished it in sticky silence and have been very close ever since. I was looking forward to seeing her again. Hoped I'd have some time with her once the job was done.

A stewardess interrupted my reverie with lunch. A tiny steak in a sauce of some sort. I tried it dubiously. Ugh! How anyone can make steak taste like plastic is a secret known only to airline caterers! Then the guy in the seat ahead lit up a truly evil cigar. I sighed, it was going to be a long trip. I pushed away the unappetizing food and dug my latest sci-fi (a new Heinlein) out of my bag and tried to ignore the world.

Two plane changes and many long, stiff, hours later I saw the coastline of Belize approaching and watched the reef pass below us. Turquoise water so clear I could see the coral beneath it. Mangrove islets edged with white sand. The runway came in sight at last.

My favorite immigration officer told me the latest gossip while we waited for the customs officer to turn up. Twenty minutes later I walked out into the scorching sun and chose a taxi driver out of the pack that beseiged me.

Two years ago the operator in charge of South America was killed by a ricochetting bullet that went through his eyes and out the back of his head. The second in command panicked. I took over and finished the operation. When I got back the Boss and the head shrink had long talks with me. I was given temporary command of a couple of operations in South America. When it became obvious that I'd found my niche, it was made official and I've been in charge of South America, which includes Central America and the Caribbean, ever since. (Though any of the seven regional operators can be pulled out of their areas to do a job in some other part of the world if their particular skills are needed for some reason, or, like my last job, if the operator there winds up dead or missing.) That job two years ago that I had to finish had been in the eastern edge of Guatemala, along the Belizean border, though it had nothing to do with Belize. That was as close as I'd come to working in Belize before, Belize being a remarkably peaceable country. Well, that was about to change, not that Belize had anything to do with Jedson either, except as a vacation spot.

I wondered about that too—why leave one Caribbean holiday resort for another if he wanted a vacation? His visit probably had a lot more to do with establishing a new casino / kidnap ring than with any personal vacation. Belize is strategically located in Central America and Moscow would undoubtedly like its own private set-up here.

I sighed and tried to forget Jedson and watch the scenery instead.

Chapter Three

BELIZE

THE TAXI turned up the hibiscus-lined driveway leading to my brother's lovely sprawling ranch house. The front yard was a blaze of color. Sarah's parrot squawked from the porch. The dogs, two dobermans and an alsatian, barked ferociously until they saw who it was. (Stealing is a major problem in Belize and all farmhouses have a pack of dogs.) Then Sarah, all round brown curves and dimples, rushed out and tried ineffectually to get the dogs to behave. She ushered me into the house, closing the door on them. She gets upset when I arrive unannounced—always worried that the house isn't neat or something. I assured her it was lovely, it always was, and explained I hadn't had time to let them know I was coming—unexpected vacation.

The twins arrived with a crash and much shouting for Aunt Tessa to see how big they were—almost grown up! Identical four-year olds, brown eyes, brown hair, and brown skin, they were christened with the unlikely names of Angela and Charity. As they are impossible to tell apart, and inseparable, everyone just calls them the Twins. Certainly so far their personalities have given no hint of being either angelic, or charitable—their most common announcements being, ''That's MINE!'' and ''I'm gonna HIT you!''

Sarah dispatched them to find Ken and Gayle and

went off to make tea. I went out on the porch and collapsed in a hammock. The Twins got back as Sarah and the tea arrived, helped themselves liberally to the cookies, and then piled into the hammock with me over Sarah's objections. I didn't mind the Twins and the cookies, my suit was beyond salvage anyway, but I objected when they tried to add one of the dogs to the pile as well.

Gayle and Ken came around the corner of the house together and I struggled out of the hammock to hug them both. Christ! Gayle must have grown four inches in the six months since I'd seen her! I let the waves of family and dogs and farm news wash over me. As always I asked a lot of questions and answered as few as possible. When Sarah started in on the when-was-I-going-to-settle-down-and-raise-a-family routine I gave in to the Twins' demands and distributed presents all around, take-apart toys for the Twins, a cookbook for Sarah, some new tapes for Ken, and a "grown-up pearl" necklace for Gayle.

Dinner was beautiful. Sarah, like many Belizean women, is an excellent cook. Thick steaks, their own beef, with a hot Mexican sauce that could have cooked the meat by itself. Sweet potatoes, rice, and beans cooked with coconut milk, onions, and hot peppers, and a salad from their garden. The mango season had been a long one this year so there were mangos and great wheels of fresh pineapple for dessert. All home-grown. Then Sarah came out of the kitchen, beaming, carrying a just-baked coconut pie! I nearly foundered after that meal.

I got up early the next morning and went for a walk. Ken was working on the tractor when I got back. A big, heavily built man with sun-streaked hair and a weathered face, no one would ever mistake him for anything other than a farmer. I helped him get the manifold off before we went into breakfast, a bit greasy but hungry. Ken and Sarah went into Belmopan for supplies later in the morning and I went along and took a stroll around the town.

The mailbox produced an invitation to a beating of the retreat at Airport Camp (the same one I had considered killing Jedson at, back at Headquarters, until I decided otherwise). They invited me along and I accepted happily. It was Thursday, the retreat was Saturday. A bit short notice, but the Belize postal service is known for sometimes delivering invitations after the event is over.

I did nothing toward Jedson's assassination for the next few days. Just worked on the farm, went riding with Gayle after school and renewed old friendships. Wanted to see if anyone seemed unduly interested in my activities but I saw nothing to make me suspicious.

Saturday morning the rain was bucketing down. Sarah and I stayed indoors and made jam from their guavas. Gayle helped us and then read to the Twins, in an effort to keep them out from under our feet. She and an older friend of hers would babysit while we were at the retreat. Sarah and I decided on what to wear and departure time. It was still raining when we left at 5 o'clock. The drive was supposed to take an hour and a half and cocktails were at 6:30, but a flat tire put us into Airport Camp a few minutes late. Ken showed our invitation to the guard at the gate who checked it against a list, then waved us through. We went around and parked in front of the officers' mess. The brigadier and his wife greeted us as we entered. The mess president started to steer us to the bar but wound up steering Sarah only, as Ken and I disappeared in opposite directions to wash off the mud we'd acquired from changing the tire.

We were handed large glasses of Pimms on our return. Pimms is an English drink which tastes like weak lemonade and dishwater. A few Pimms later and you can barely crawl let alone stand up. They are nasty, insipid-tasting drinks that, at least after the mess stewards get finished with them, leap up and clobber you over the head when you least expect it. I exchanged mine for a rum and coke at the first opportunity.

There is nothing to do at a cocktail party except stand around and get drunk and talk to people you won't see again till the next cocktail party, and don't want to then. That is, unless you are a single female at a cocktail party at the officers' mess. No other experience can beat it for making a woman feel like the most glamorous, exotic, and totally desirable woman in the world. Single females are few and far between, and only a handful of the thousand or so troops stationed in Belize have their wives with them. I was almost sorry when it was time for the retreat to begin.

Since I wasn't trying to shoot Jedson here after all, I went out well escorted by a phalanx of officers all telling me to watch out for the mud on the path. A major took one arm and a colonel the other to help me over the rough spot, and so I was ensconced between them in the front row just down from the British high commissioner. Jedson walked in a moment later surrounded by several Belizean businessmen and a couple of hard types that looked very out of place. Wondered if he had any more body-guards elsewhere. The pictures I'd been shown had failed to convey the feeling of power. They'd shown a big man of mixed racial ancestry in his early forties who looked hard. In the flesh the hardness wasn't so obvious. A touch of gray in the close-cropped kinky hair. Large eyes and sensual lips. The man emanated vitality and power. No wonder he'd been chosen by Cuba. I wondered what Havana thought of his expensive suit and the solid gold watch that looked big enough to eat off of.

Then the retreat began and I was swept up by the beauty and pageantry of it. A full-dress retreat by the British Forces is a page out of a gallant history that can't be seen in many places anymore. The uniforms were magnificent but why the lads didn't drop dead from heatstroke I'll never know. True, the sun was down, but I was still sweating in my thin sleeveless gown and the men on either side of me were sweltering in long sleeves and ties. The leader led the band out across the field stepping high in time to the music. When they reached the center of the field, they wheeled and came straight toward us, peeling away at the last moment. The strain showed on those boys' faces. They would have died rather than play a wrong note. There is something to be said for tradition and a history of honor and loyalties that stretches back so far.

Then the band finished its maneuvers and withdrew to the side of the field. Now it was the turn of the pipes and drums. The infantry regiment out at the time was a Scots one, hence the pipers, in their kilts, that came striding down the field, bagpipes skirling. Fascinating sound. I love to hear them. If you close your eyes the sound conjures up the wild hills and the swirling driven mists that bore the pipes. The sound seemed out of place in the middle of a steaming mangrove swamp full of biting insects. The sandflies were out in force, too. I thankfully borrowed some repellent that someone passed around.

When the pipers finished, the band came back on the field and they did some joint maneuvers, then the bandmasters asked permission to quit the field and the retreat was over. Too quickly for me. It seemed a long ride back to the farm.

Monday morning we got ready to go into Belize City. I told Ken I'd stay there for a few days, and look up some friends, maybe spend a day or two at the cays. Sarah reminded me that I was invited to the British High Commissioner's house for cocktails Saturday evening. I assured her I'd be back in time—you don't just ''not turn up'' at such things. I needed a few days on my own away from the farm. There were a couple of details to see to before I killed Jedson.

Ken and Sarah dropped me at the Bellevue Hotel where I always stay when I'm in town. I'd reserved a room by phone from Belmopan the previous week. (The telephone system is restricted to the main towns. Outlying villages usually have a radio / phone linkup from the local storeowner's home. Farmers and other country people do without, no great loss in my opinion.) I booked in and dumped my bags in my room. The bag with my gun in it, I'd left at the farm. Didn't care to risk having it stolen. My knife and garrote were in my purse. Phoned Dennis, who I always rent a vehicle from as soon as I arrive in the city, and arranged for him to drop off a Landrover that afternoon. Fortunately, a Landrover is what I usually rent, and I regularly stay elsewhere than the farm during my visits to Belize. Nothing to seem out of the ordinary to anyone.

I went out for a stroll around town and to buy some toothpaste before meeting Ken and Sarah for a gorgeous lobster lunch.

Later that evening I drifted into the bar. I wanted an invitation up to Airport Camp and a lot of military personnel frequented the Bellevue Bar. Unfortunately, the place was dead. Monday night is usually dead. The bar is really several interconnecting rooms. As you come in, there is a place for the band and a group of tables on your left. Straight ahead and on a higher level, is one end of a long curving bar. Lovely high-backed bar seats. To the left of the far end of the bar is another area of tables, also raised, and a piano. Beyond that is a dance floor just visible through an archway behind the band. When it gets too crowded, people dance in front of the band as well. Old weapons hang from the walls between carved wooden plaques of Mayan inspiration. Mayan designs also inspired the deep bas-relief mural that covers the wall behind the band. No band tonight, though, and only one other customer.

I ordered a drink and talked to the barman. We'd about exhausted the weather, his family, his wife's family, and the bar business by the time an RAF pilot I knew from previous trips showed up. Name of Steve. A couple of his buddies turned up half an hour later and we all proceeded to get a wee bit drunk. Somebody started playing the piano. Someone else started "Roll Me Over, Lay Me Down and Do It Again" and we all joined in. All in all Monday evening picked up a bit but I turned in early. But not before wrangling an invitation to the film at the sergeants' mess the following night.

The morning dawned hot and muggy. I spent four hours on the telephone trying to get through to my bank manager to check that Paul's hospital bills were being taken care of. Paul's bills were mounting the way only hospital bills involving specialists can. A good thing I'm well paid.

I should have spent the afternoon visiting people to stay in character, but I holed up in my air-conditioned room with my Heinlein that I still hadn't had a chance to finish. Even the air conditioner was finding it hard going. There was a rapidly-growing puddle on the floor. I threw a towel over it and retreated onto the bed until time for dinner.

Ate quickly and went to get ready for the evening. I use British Army fatigues for bush clothes, use their jungle boots as well. Somebody'd once given me an old camouflage cap. I'd brought them all along including a webbing belt and canteen pouch. Unpacked them and put them in a shopping bag. Got dressed, red embroidered skirt and a white halter top, and combed out my hair. It would be awfully hot but I always wear it down for the evening. My knife and garrote were still in my purse. I stepped outside. My clothes wilted instantly and I retreated and put my hair up after all. Went down to the Landrover with my skirt sticking damply to my legs at each step. Tucked my shopping bag into one of the lockable compartments under the seats in the back.

By the time I negotiated the 15 miles of mud, chuckholes, and insane drivers between Belize City and Airport Camp, I was thinking how stupid my ghost was going to feel explaining to the Boss that I couldn't do the job because I'd been killed in a traffic accident involving a cow, a taxi driver, and the military police Landrover.

When I finally arrived, shaken but in one piece, I was told to wait at the guardroom until they got Steve on the phone and he came to collect me. I was also handed a book to fill in: my name, address, nationality, vehicle license number, time of arrival, and where I was going on camp. Felt tempted to put down my real destination, but refrained. We got in just as the film started. Steve had reserved one of the few comfortable seats for me and left a buddy defending it with his life. I accepted gratefully and settled back to enjoy the film, nothing I could do till it was over anyway. It was a most unconvincing sci-fi.

Once the movie was finished and a group of us were sitting around with drinks in our hands, I steered the conversation to Landrovers, easy enough since I was renting one. The great majority of men in this world love talking about cars. Army men are no different. And if you've made sure there are a couple of guys from REME (Royal Electrical and Mechanical Engineers) in the circle, no one is going to get the conversation onto anything else. By the end of an hour I knew which Landrover I was going to steal. No point in stealing just any Landrover, I might get a lemon. Much rather steal a good one. But it had to be somewhere out of sight and easily stolen. The REME workshop was right at the back end of the camp, not far from the airport and it was deserted at night. I'd just been told which vehicles were ready for use and which one had a cracked head. Can't steal the brigadier's, too much fuss would be made. Radar's would be ideal. They have two anyway and they don't really need any as they only use them for running around camp and into town. REME had just finished overhauling one of Radar's that evening.

I left around 11:30. Waved to the young sentry at the gate and drove out their road onto the main highway leading toward Belize City. But half a mile down the road I turned into the road to the airport. About a quarter of a mile down, there is a track that leads off to the left. Used to be a house back in a ways, but it's long deserted. I pulled in just far enough to be out of sight from the road. Changed into my old army clothes. Pulled my cap down as far as I could, which wasn't as far as I would've liked—my hair held it up a bit—and walked back to the road.

The roads to the Airport Camp and to the airport itself are roughly half a mile apart where they meet the highway, but then they angle towards each other and the back of Airport Camp virtually touches the airport. There are a number of gun emplacements protecting the airfield and several dirt tracks connect them with the camp itself. Where Airport Camp faces the highway, it is guarded by sentries and concertina wire, and God knows what else, but the airfield itself is almost considered part of the camp and the dirt tracks wander through freely.

At night one figure in fatigues and boots looks like any other— I hoped. I'd been careful to wear no perfume and virtually no lipstick either. (Most lipstick is perfumed—eyeshadow is not.) When I changed clothes, I wiped off any remaining makeup. Some of the boys in the forces are only 18 and 19. Their voices aren't any lower than mine. And Bobby taught me long ago to imitate a variety of British accents. I should pass any cursory check. It was late enough, with luck I wouldn't meet anyone anyway. So—I walked up the road to the airfield and cut down the first track toward camp as if I had a perfect right to be there.

Unfortunately, that track led to a gun—not the camp. Hastily back-tracked before anyone noticed me, and tried again. I must have wandered around in the mud for an hour before I finally recognized the first camp buildings. Nearly fell into Radar's bloody fishpond! Some bored soul a few years ago had decided to landscape his rather distant and dismal post. The result was a thatch roof over a cement floor with a bamboo-walled bar in the center. And a fishpond, backed by a ridge of plants. Radar became famous for their parties but I never had thought much of the pond. In the dark, a thatch roof looks very much like the palms from which it is made, if you only see a small part of it, the rest being hidden by trees. I stepped over a little ridge and barely stopped in time. At least I now knew where I was. Unfortunately, Radar is manned around the clock, so I backed up and stole silently along the side of their huts. Silently, that is, until I stepped on a beer bottle and measured my length on a pile of empty bottles and cans. The noise was appalling. I remembered to curse in a British accent. Somebody inside swore at "tha' drunken sod Billy." I blessed drunken Billy whoever he might be and tried to think what he'd be most likely to do after falling and being sworn at when drunk. Took a chance and pitched the first bottle I laid hands on in the general direction of the voice and followed it with some comments on the voice's ancestry. Apparently that was what Billy would have done as laughter was followed by silence. Still mumbling in what I hoped was a convincing manner, I got out of there. I was beginning to wonder about the wisdom of this venture.

The dirt track from Radar led to the end of the tarmac road which I was very glad to see. Five minutes later a Landrover came down it. No time to disappear anywhere, so I kept walking head down and shoulders hunched, looking, I hoped, like a tired soldier coming off duty. Threw a salute as they passed remembering only at the last second to salute British style instead of US style. God! What a mistake to make! My nerves were dancing jigs by this time—and these guys were on *my* side, in theory at least!

Eventually found the REME workshops only to find some zealous idiot still working over a greasy-looking item on a bench. To my disgusted eye it seemed he had enough lights on to provide for a small town. Maybe he was scared of the dark. It had begun to rain by then, but not enough to discourage the mosquitos. I sat in the bushes fuming and getting wetter and more thoroughly bitten

by the minute. I regretted bitterly my decision not to bring repellent, but it has a strong, easily recognized smell. The minutes
dragged. The rain settled in earnest. The mechanic finished at last
only to dig out another bit of something and start on that. Looked
like he was there for the night. I couldn't wait any longer. It was
pushing 1:30 A.M. and I still had a lot to do before daylight, which
comes about 5:30 A.M. in Belize that time of year.

So I took off my boot and filled my sock with muddy sand,
tamping it down well. Took my other boot off as well, checked to
make sure no one was in sight, and circled around just beyond the
cone of light. The side of the shed was in deep shadow. When I
reached the corner I dropped flat and poked my head around just
far enough to see that he was still bending over the bench. A slight
motion at ground level is far less likely to be noticed than one at
head level. I stood up and sprinted across the ten feet separating
us. The rain drowned any noise my bare feet might have made. He
never knew he'd been hit. Sand in a sock makes a very effective
cosh. I dragged him into the workshop and laid him against the
wall. He'd rest there peacefully for a few hours, then wake up with
one hell of a headache but nothing more. (Knowing how hard and
where to hit for what effect is an art which Bobby's skilled in and
enjoys teaching.)

Dumped the sand from my sock and washed the rest out in a
puddle. Put my boots back on. Now, to steal a Landrover. I picked
out Radar's insignia on the door of the one on the end. To my
surprise the key from the rental Landrover worked. I'd expected
to have to hot wire it but decided I might as well try the easy way
first. Checked that the spare was okay and that the tank was full,
swiped a tow bar out of the brigadier's Landrover and threw it in
the back, then got in and drove off. Didn't see a soul on the way
back to where I'd left my rental Landrover and only got lost twice.

Pulled in beside the other Landrover and spent the next 40

minutes jockeying Landrovers around trying to get the blasted tow bar hooked up correctly. Should have taken a tow rope instead, *much* simpler! Praying no one came along—I'd have a hell of a time trying to talk my way out at this point and I definitely did not want to leave any dead bodies lying around. Those tow bars look so simple. Maybe they are on a flat road in day light if you've used one before. I ran out of suitable vocabulary and undamaged knuckles early on. By the time I finished, the ground was so torn up over such a large area that I figured nobody would ever figure out what had happened there let alone connect it with a stolen Landrover. I scraped Radar's insignia off—someone might wonder what they were doing out of camp at that hour.

Once I was out on the main road I should be safe. At least I hoped no one would think anything of a forces Landrover towing a civvy one in the middle of the night. Helpful sorts these army blokes. And rental Landrovers are renowned for breaking down.

The Western Highway is deserted after 10:00 P.M. on week nights and I never saw another car once I left the city. The rain stopped. I made the 50 miles between Belize City and Belmopan in under 2 hours. Not bad when you consider that a canvas-back, short-wheel forces model weighs considerably less than a long-wheel-base, all-metal civilian one does. I had to stop a time or so to keep the engine from overheating. At the Belmopan junction, I turned south on the Hummingbird Highway, bypassing Belmopan, and went another 8 miles. Slowed down till I was barely creeping along, hunting for the logging track I knew was there. Saw it. Put the Landrover in four-wheel drive, low-range, and eased off the main road. The bush closed overhead immediately. As soon as the rental vehicle was well off the road, I got out and took it off the tow before driving the one I'd stolen farther in. The Landrover struggled and fought its way through a quarter of a mile of thick mud. Figured it was well out of sight there. The track didn't look like it had been used this year, so with luck no one would come along before next dry season.

I slogged back, changed clothes again and tried to wipe the worst of the mud off my hands and legs. Gave it up as a bad job. Reversed the rental Landrover back onto the highway, no mean trick considering the angle and the mud. The wheels spun furiously, slinging mud for 50 feet in all directions as the back end started sliding sideways. Stopped and pulled forward or rather, tried to. Back wheels stuck. Rocked it back and forth gaining an inch or so each time till one wheel finally bit on something solid— kept going—free. I was wet, muddy, mosquito-bitten and fuming again. To hell with it! Pulled well forward and took a running start. The truck leaped and bounced backwards up over the lip onto the highway, slewing around wildly as the muddy tires hit the wet pavement. Fortunately, no one was coming by just then. Got it pointing the right direction and started the long drive back to the city.

Got in around five A.M., and pounded on the door until the night porter finally woke up and let me in. He took in the hour and my disheveled appearance, grinned, and asked me if I'd had a good night. I winked at him and said I had indeed. Staggered up to my room, took a hot shower, and collapsed in bed.

Ventured forth the next day in time for lunch and did a bit of shopping on the way back to the Belleview. A gallon of dark blue paint, two small tins of paint, one white and one black, a "No Trespassing" sign, a large paint brush and a small one, some turpentine, scissors, and a screwdriver.

A shop attendant I didn't recognize grinned at me and said, "Da wan reel pritty soldja-bwy a dun see yo wi' las ni'."

Huh? Oh, Steve! Somehow that summed up Belize to me—a girl I'd never seen before in my life, so far as I knew, commenting on whom I was out with the night before! Sometimes Belize was a little *too* friendly! Decided the elaborate precautions I was taking were indeed called for. Once Jedson was dead, any unexplained vehicle within 10 miles of Belmopan was going to be the subject of considerable interest. A rental Landrover would stick out in retrospect like the proverbial sore thumb and would be traced to me immediately. And I wasn't going to risk involving Ken by using one of the farm trucks.

I made an early start the next morning. The hotel had packed a lunch for me the night before as I was supposedly going for a hike up the Sibun river. I wore my old hiking clothes and said I'd be back in time for dinner—telling them to save the biggest lobster for me. Belize is a rarity these days, an uncrowded place that isn't totally inhospitable. You can drive for long stretches along any of the three main roads in the country without seeing a building. Just miles of coastal savannahs that eventually give way to miles of jungle. Beautiful.

As the Landrover lurched and crashed from one chuckhole to the next, I reminded myself that the horrible state of what passes for roads in Belize is part of why the country isn't crowded. I pulled in the logging track until I was out of sight of the highway and got out. It was a beautiful sunny morning and I thoroughly enjoyed painting my stolen Landrover. About 10:00 the blackflies descended on me but I had repellent this time. Practically took a bath in the stuff before they left me alone. The bugs divide up a 24-hour period very well: sandflies and mosquitos all night, mosquitos in the early morning until the blackflies take over for the day. They're helped out by a liberal sprinkling of deerflies; just as they're getting tired it's time for half an hour of large loud horseflies that give a truly impressive bite. By then it's dark and the mosquitoes and sandflies are back. Sometimes I wonder why I'm so fond of Belize.

Finished the Landrover by 1:00. Took my picnic lunch over to a reject log abandoned by the side of the track. Lunch tasted slightly of paint and turpentine, but other than that was quite respectable. A brilliant, iridescent-blue damsel fly came and sat on my knee. An ant crawled up over my tennis shoe and bit me on the ankle. I squished it with my other shoe and that scared away the damsel fly. A Mot-Mot bird "tocked" in the distance and I could see several smaller brightly colored birds flitting around in the undergrowth. A shiny green beetle walked by waving its antennae and I felt utterly at peace with the world. After a while a whole colony of ants found me and hastened my decision to get back to work.

The Landrover was a nice nondescript dark blue now but it needed a new license place. I'd removed the distinctive black-on-yellow forces plate before I started painting. I couldn't just repaint it as civilian plates are larger than forces ones. I got out the 'No Trespassing' sign I'd bought. It was flexible but waterproof. The scissors and two coats of white paint produced quite a respectable blank license plate. I buried the paint cans I was finished with well back in the bush while waiting for the "license plate" to dry. When it was, I added a black border and a suitable combination of letters and numbers. When that dried as well, I screwed it back where the original had been and rubbed a bit of mud over it, especially around the edges, and checked out my handiwork. Perfect. It would pass any but a very close inspection.

I started the Landrover up and let the engine run while I buried the rest of the bits and pieces and cleaned the paint off me and out of my clothes as best I could. Then I left my newly painted Landrover where it was and got back in my legal one, the rental one. I just had time enough to drive down to the Sibun River, where I was supposed to have been all day, for a swim. I walked upstream a ways and went in fully clothed. Coming back a bit waterlogged after a day hiking up a river was logical, but coming back smelling of paint and turpentine wouldn't be. I clung to a rock and let the current wash over and through my clothes while I watched the sunlight dancing on the water. It felt beautiful. I was sorry to leave—would much prefer to have spent the day hiking; still, I was pleased with the day's results.

The lobster that evening was superb. Went into the bar afterwards. Half of Airport Camp must have decided to come to the Bellevue for the dance that night. The combo was tuning up and the place was already full by 9:00. I looked in—the air conditioners were already barely coping. It would be a real steambath soon, and most of the soldiers looked like kids. 'Nough to make me feel like someone's grandmother. I left. Went to bed early, but it didn't work.

It was a long and bad night. The sort you can't afford in this business. When your mind won't turn off and insists on dragging up those things you can only stay sane by pushing out of your mind: the time I didn't take a garrotte with me and had to use a piece of radio aerial. Of course it couldn't cut, only strangle. I must've gotten a bad grip. The sentry refused to die for a very, very long time. Cut me up pretty bad before he did and left his knife in my belly. . . . The time I threw a hand grenade just as an old woman darted out in the street. . . . The day I returned to base camp after several days absence and the stench met me before I saw what was left of the backup team.

Eventually I dreamed I was back in my house, in my own bed. My safe house. But something was moving in the dark at the foot of the bed. I didn't want to look. When I did I could see the shadowy outline of a bear. And another bear. My house that the bears couldn't find. But they had. I could hear them laughing softly to themselves. I'd been a fool to think they could never find me. And I would pay for being a fool. The bears came closer, swaying and shoving against the foot of my bed. I could see them clearly now as I cowered at the head of the bed. They reared up, towering over me. One held a blackjack in one paw and a set of clamps and wires in the other. The second one had a scalpel and a syringe. Their faces were massive, faces that had never known the meaning of "pity." I tried to hide under the covers but the bed turned into a stainless steel table. Steel fingers grew around my ankles and wrists. Stainless steel bands sealed around my throat and chest.

There would be no rescue this time. No one would come and carry the shell that the bears hadn't yet destroyed back to the safe places. In the past the doctors had been able to coax the pieces that were in hiding out with promises of no more pain, promises of revenge. And when those bits of me came back the doctors patted themselves on the back and said, "She's alive and well." When they gave me a gun and I could still shoot, they smiled even more and said, "She's alive and well and functioning." But they didn't know. They knew I hadn't told the bears anything they wanted to know but they didn't know the bears had cut out bits and put them in a stainless steel jar labeled with my name. Now the bears had found me again. This time I knew they would cut me up in little pieces when they were through and put all of me in the stainless steel jars. And I knew with a corrosive horror that by the time they did, I would be glad. They had all the time in the world before that. The bears loomed closer as I struggled frantically and uselessly. I couldn't stand it again. Closer, and the table laughed as it tightened the bands that held me immobile. One bear began to fasten the wires to my nipples. The other leaned over to me to do the same to my ears. Its breath reeked of a thousand years of horrors.

I woke, sweat pouring off me in rivers, my throat raw from silent screams. I got the light switch on the third try. I was shaking so hard I had trouble getting to the shower. Turned it on full cold and stood under it for what seemed an eternity. Eventually, after I'd mostly stopped shaking, I got out and dried myself, trying not to touch the tiny scars on my nipples and ears—and the inner folds of my vagina. I went back to the bed but I knew that if I tried to sleep again that night the bears would be waiting. Alcohol wouldn't help either. Nothing would. I turned on the rest of the lights in both rooms, sat up in bed, and tried to read for the remainder of the night.

Though it sounds strange to say it, nightmares are one of the biggest hazards an operator has to deal with. We have to be able to think in our line of work, and once you can think, you have a certain amount of imagination—enough for nightmares. Your conscious mind can rationalize and weigh one life against twenty, but your subconscious doesn't. Your conscious mind also re-presses terror and pain memories. We all have nightmares at times. But if you let them get a hold on you, you're through. Too many tormented nights and you're exhausted and jump at every sound. And then you're dead. As simple as that.

But this nightmare was more than just a nightmare—too much of it was real and the memory of the reality prevented me from reading for a long time. I kept remembering pain. Pain that filled the world. Following . . . swelling relentlessly. Then darkness. Numbness. Nothingness. But the bloated, obscene pain still there . . . waiting . . . screams tearing through dark agony, back behind where the pain-that-filled the-world was. Pain scorching ahead, trying to swallow my mind, drag it back, forcing it into the body that couldn't escape . . . No blackness anymore, only pain. And the screams I couldn't shut out . . . me screaming.

I managed to push those memories away, but then the other memories came in neat orderly fashion—the rescue, the psycho-therapy—everyone being oh-so-careful-what-they-said-around-me. And finally the weeks of planning and carrying out my retaliation. The last memories were almost as bad as the first. I'd rather not know I am capable of that sort of savagery no matter what the excuse. Shooting would have been sufficient.

I felt ancient and brittle the next day—finally slept awhile in the afternoon. Got back to the farm with barely enough time to grab a sandwich and change clothes. I felt annoyed with the world in general and snapped at the Twins. Even snapped at Gayle for absolutely no reason and felt even worse when I saw the hurt in her face. Chose a long Guatemalan skirt with an Ecuadorean blouse, and my favorite pre-Columbian style gold jewelry, jaguar shapes with tiny rubies for eyes. Checked to make sure both the knife and garrotte were safe in the false bottom of my purse and I was ready to go. Still in a perfectly foul mood, which worsened during the drive. By the time I got there I knew I was either going to get very drunk or do something stupid or both. I hate myself when I get moods like that—I have to live with the hangover and / or the consequences the next day!

The British High Commissioner's house is a two-story building flanked by tennis courts and a swimming pool. We gave our names at the guardhouse at the bottom of the drive and were waved in.

We went in and greeted High Commissioner Brent-Halsey and his wife. Many of the faces I recognized from the retreat. More people were here from the various foreign consulates, including several from the U.S. Embassy, and there were more Belizean dignitaries. And of course only a few British officers. Thank God a major I'd met at the retreat rescued me from Sarah, her mother, the new colonel's wife, and some stout, overbearing old cow I'd managed to avoid being formally introduced to.

Another minute and I'd have said something I'd regret. Lobster pieces on toothpicks to dip in a choice of sauces, tiny sausage rolls, cubes of fresh pineapple and melon, and various gooey things on small pieces of very thin bread. I tried them all before settling on the lobster each time it came around. Immaculate waiters in immaculate jackets kept our glasses filled. I emptied mine far too often and can't even remember getting into the truck, let alone the drive home. I do, unfortunately, remember waking up the next day.

Oh God, my head ached. My stomach lurched and I tried to loosen my tongue. My mouth tasted like a vulture's crotch. Why had I ever drunk so much? No way was I getting up yet. Didn't care if the world came to an end. I wasn't getting up. Oh God, never again. Till the next time a nasty little jerk in the corner of my mind whispered. Shut up, I'm dying. My room felt hot and sticky and I was still wearing my evening clothes—must be late morning. I can just imagine my sister-in-law's expression. Forget it. She won't be any more horrified if I get up in the afternoon than she will be if I get up this late anyway—well—not much.

When I finally crawled downstairs it was to find Ken and Sarah in the middle of a furious argument which they immediately tried to drag me into. I hate getting involved in family arguments, in the first place. Something I try to avoid like the plague. In the second place, I still had a truly horrendous hangover. And third, I couldn't remember ever doing a job where my private life intruded before and I don't ever want to again. Nieces and four-year-old Twins and parties are all very well and good and, indeed, very enjoyable, but not on a bloody job. And time was getting short.

I tried to ignore the fight that had sent the children and the dogs fleeing outdoors. All I wanted to do was to get a cup of tea and go back to bed and die. Ken tried to get me to side with him.

I sighed, ''Look, I haven't a clue what this is all about, I only just came in at the middle of it. Something to do with churches and Gayle I gather, but how about somebody clueing me in?''

Sarah looked furious. ''Don't bother. She doesn't even go to church. Look at her! She's only just dragged herself up from last night and it's the middle of the afternoon! Really, I don't understand why you allow her to set such a disgraceful example in front of the child. . . .''

"You will NOT speak about my sister like that! Her life is her own, unlike mine, and what she does is *her* business. And don't forget who helped us after the hurricane—just in case you've forgotten she spent two solid weeks work'n like a dog 'n then paid all the bills we couldn't. Ah do'n remember *your* family help. . . ."

Oh shit—dragging in who helped, or didn't help, who, when, was all they needed to make it the sort of fight that nobody ever really forgets. Umm. Time to intercede—I took a deep breath and yelled, "Shut up both of you! You people were already doing a rip roaring job of fighting *before* you dragged me into it! What was the original fight about? I still want to know what Gayle has to do with churches."

Twenty minutes later I'd gotten the general gist of it. Sarah wanted Gayle to attend Sunday-school classes in Belmopan. Ken didn't want to drive all the way to Belmopan and back every Sunday. Mmm—had a feeling Gayle's riding and generally being a tomboy had a lot to do with it too. Sunday school wouldn't hurt Gayle and it seemed to me that Ken had better give in or he was going to have real trouble with Sarah. I couldn't explain to Ken that Sarah felt her role as a mother threatened by the freedom Gayle was being allowed. Better Ken should do some extra driving than Gayle have her freedom resented too much by her mother. So I amazed them both by siding with Sarah. It was the only time I've ever sided definitely with either of them in a private argument. Always tried to stay out of it before. But they both know I tend to share Ken's views of life rather than Sarah's. The argument quit due to sheer shock. I took advantage of the silence, abandoned my cup of tea, and escaped to my bedroom.

Sarah woke me with another cup of tea before dinner. She apologized, very sincerely, for misjudging me. (At which, I felt a bit guilty.) Apparently, she'd done some real soul searching while I'd been asleep and admitted to herself that she'd always been jealous of my exotic beauty and of Gayle's love for me. Jesus! That had taken a lot of guts to realize, let alone tell me. We talked for a long time and got to know each other really for the first time. Discovered she had a lot more steel to her than I'd ever guessed. I tried to make things easier with Gayle by reminding her that it's very easy to love someone you don't see very often and take for granted your parents who take care of you every day! An unspoken truce was made and I had a feeling we might even become friends someday. Have to admit I'd just stereotyped her as a farm wife before and pretty much ignored her, spending my time with Gayle and Ken—no wonder she'd resented me. Resolved to change things in the future.

Dinner was excellent, if a bit more silent than usual. I played Parcheesi with the Twins in penance while Gayle and Sarah washed up.

I went to bed when the children did. Tomorrow night was the night and I wanted to be well rested.

At breakfast I told Ken and Sarah I was going camping for a couple of days. Gayle promptly wanted to come with me. (I will never mix my personal life up in a job again, Boss or no Boss!) Ken and Sarah were concerned about my going alone. Ken even offered to take a few days off and come with me. I had one hell of a time getting out of being accompanied without hurting anyone's feelings too much. I pleaded overwork, tired nerves, a need to be alone for a few days, need to sort out some things for myself and anything else I could think of. Promised Gayle we'd go out to the reef or someplace for a while before I left.

After breakfast I dug my camping gear out of their shed and went upstairs to pack. I keep a pack, ground sheet, and miscellaneous cooking pots, etc., at the farm. Saves trying to carry it all down with me every time I come. Gayle stuck to me like glue. She was awed at the thought of my going off alone in the bush for several days. I had before, but I went through the same fuss from the family each time. In desperation, I sent Gayle down to request some thread and a needle from Sarah for me to take along. Actually, I had one in my first-aid kit, but Gayle didn't know that and I had to get her out of my room long enough for me to get out Beauty and the plastic explosive and shove them in the bottom of the pack. I couldn't think why I'd need any plastic but I put it in anyway. I follow my hunches if there's no real reason not to and occasionally even if there is. I barely had the stuff out of sight before Gayle reappeared. She must have run all the way! I sent her off to check my watch against their clock while I got my knife and garrotte out of my purse and into the pack too.

I was ready to leave by 8:30. I didn't want to be in Belmopan for at least another twelve hours but it would look extremely odd if I left on a camping trip at seven at night! I surreptitiously shoved a paperback in as well and left. Well, I left after saying goodbye to everybody except the Twins—they had to be said goodbye to about six times—and again after evicting a dog from the back of the Landrover. Got 50 feet down the drive and discovered a back tire was flat. Changed it and had to evict two dogs and one twin from the back of the Landrover, and remove the other one from the hood where she was attempting to find out what held the windshield wipers on. Not much apparently—she had one off and the second wasn't far behind. By the time I got the wipers back on, there was a dog in the back again and a twin in the driver's seat. In desperation, I used language they understood—after a quick check to see that neither Ken nor Sarah were within hearing range—I hissed theatrically, ''I'm gonna HIT you!'' Worked like a charm. Four brown eyes widened in astonishment, looked at each other, and vanished. The dogs sensed the change in atmosphere and left too. I got out of there quick before the effect wore off.

The Assassin and the Deer

When I stopped in Belmopan to get the tire repaired, I discovered a blue plastic duck under it. Twenty minutes later, with a good spare and a toy duck for company, I was on my way. I wondered if any of the other operators had ever started off on a job accompanied by one rather sticky blue duck; I doubted it somehow.

The miles went quickly, too quickly. I pulled in behind my stolen Landrover and switched off the engine. Got out and started up the stolen one, letting it run for a few minutes. Nothing more to do before dark. I settled down in the rental one—more comfortable seats—opened both doors to let the breeze through, and tried to read my book. I shared my lunch crackers and cheese with some little birds that were hopping around. The water in my canteen was already warm, tasting like plastic.

I hate waiting before a job. Any operator does. You know you should relax and rest as much as possible while you can. You can't. Looked at the toy duck and wondered for the millionth time what it would be like to have kids. Decided for the millionth and first that I wouldn't have the patience.

Jedson. It should be easy. What could go wrong?

No one had tried to kill me yet. Why not? Did whoever tried before really not know I was here?

The afternoon dragged by in inches. I curled up on the seat and tried to sleep. As soon as I gave up and decided to go for a walk instead, it started to pour. Every bug for fifty yards around took refuge from the rain in the Landrover with me. The rain cleared off and the mosquitos descended for half an hour before it was time to go.

I backed out first the rental Landrover and then the stolen one. I got them hooked up considerably faster than on Wednesday night. Other way around this time. The rental one pulled the other with no strain. No one would think anything of one civvy Landrover, rental or otherwise, pulling another civvy one. The Forces auctioned off their old ones regularly and there are lots of repainted and relicensed former army Landrovers running around the back roads of Belize. I just didn't want to do it in daylight when someone might recognize me. I drove another ten miles to the Sibun River. Pulled the rental one off the road and parked it on a gravel bar beside the river. Didn't matter who saw it there, I was supposed to be camping up that way anyhow. Transferred my pack to my stolen Landrover and headed back to Belmopan and Jedson.

Chapter Four

THE BAT GOD
RULES

I WAS DRIVING too fast. Slowed down. No point in rushing. My heartbeat was too fast too. I tried to slow it by taking long, deep breaths. Holding each one, letting it out in miserly fashion and waiting before drawing the next. It works anytime except just before a job. Once the days, or weeks, of planning are finally over and the time for action is coming, I'm so tightly wound I swear I'd shatter if I were dropped. The adrenaline is there—and nothing to use it yet. My stomach knots itself around my backbone and it is a real effort to unclench my teeth enough to speak. Driving too fast again. It's beyond fear or anticipation or anything else. It is the time before I kill or am killed.

By 9:00 P.M. the children should be off the streets. There would still be people wandering around then, but the moon would only begin rising by 10:00. Yesterday, after considerable mental debate, I decided I preferred more people about and a dark night, to fewer people and brilliant moonlight. A toss-up really—there would be street lights anyhow, but the more people walking and driving about the less the Landrover would stand out. Also, I wanted to shoot Jedson from outside, not have to go in and get him in his bed. I could always do that later if I had to—if there were just too many people around before he went to bed.

I stopped several miles before the Belmopan turnoff. Got Beauty out of the pack and laid her, still packed in her stock, on the seat beside me. Changed into my night clothes next. I wasn't expecting any infrared scanner but my clothes are dull black, close-fitting but extremely comfortable, and the hood covers all but my eyes if I so wish. Even hair or the back of your neck can reflect light and give a position away. I left the hood down for the moment. Put my jungle boots on. They are canvas and rubber so they don't reflect either. They're not as quiet to walk in as tennis shoes but they don't pull off if you're running and sink a foot in thick mud.

I slipped the garrote into the large inside pocket in the front of my shirt. Pulled the sleeve up on my left arm, strapped the sheath to it and slid the knife home. I didn't expect to use either weapon tonight, but I like to cover as many bets as possible.

On the same theory I took the plastic explosive, detonator, etc., and my flashlight out of the pack and put them between the seats, where they were out of sight but easy to get to. The only drawback to using a canvas-backed Landrover was that there was no way I could lock away the pack. I'd just have to hope no one stole it. On second thought, it might be a lot safer to hide it someplace and pick it up later, so I turned around and drove back down the road to a small bridge, glorified culvert really, that I knew I could find again easily and shoved the pack under it. Not brilliant but better than risking it being stolen. That used up the extra time I'd gained by driving too fast.

I entered Belmopan at 9:00 exactly. The residential streets are all dead-end streets that branch off of feeder roads. I parked on the feeder road, behind a white van, just beyond the street, which led to the home Jedson was staying in. I made sure I was close enough to his street so no one could park me in. I didn't want to have to back and fill before I could leave—I would be in a hurry. Neither had I any intention of getting trapped in a dead-end street.

Voices sounded from the closest house. A radio played nearby. A woman disappeared into a house on the corner of the next street. No one else in sight. I'd parked as close alongside the monsoon drain as possible. Grabbed Beauty and climbed over the gear shifts to the passenger's seat, cracked the door open and dropped down into the drain. The cement sides angled down for about three feet, then were straight for the last 18 inches or so. Roughly 4 feet wide at the top and 2 across the bottom. I crouched down and ran around the corner and 50 yards or so down on Jedson's side of the road— as long as no one looked directly into the drain, I was for all practical purposes invisible. Then a door opened somewhere on the other side of the road and there were sudden loud voices. A crosswalk spanned the drain about ten feet ahead of me and a cat shot out of the far side as I dove under it. The voices came closer— laughter—shoes on the street, then car doors slammed and they drew away after final goodbyes. No sound of anyone else close by, so I poked my head out and took a look around. I was not quite halfway to Jedson's borrowed house, borrowed from a patron of Jedson's casinos who happened to be in the U.S.A. at the moment. Rumor had it the man was a drug dealer but anyone who could afford casinos regularly would be suspected of *something* illegal. Personally, at that moment I didn't care as long as there were no unexpected family members still in the house.

I ran, still crouching, till I judged I was getting close, stopped by another crosswalk and looked again. Three houses yet to go. A street light directly in front of his house shone into the drain beside another crosswalk. Not that I had really intended to walk up the front walk. I climbed out beside my crosswalk. Fortunately, like many tropical towns, Belmopan goes in for hedges and shrubbery of all sorts.

I stopped under the low hanging branches of a casaurina tree at the back of the yard adjoining Jedson's to assemble Beauty. I was beginning to feel uneasy although as soon as I had parked, all the tensed-up-before-a-job-feeling went, as I had known it would. When I actually start the stalk, I concentrate totally on what I'm doing. Once my body has a use for that adrenaline I feel perfectly calm. But this was different. Any operator who survives more than one or two assignments either has, or develops, a sixth sense. Maybe a seventh and eighth as well. Just luck runs out after a couple of jobs. And I felt uneasy. Very uneasy. I stared at every bush in Jedson's yard. There could be half an army in there for all I could see.

It was a muggy night and I was sweating lightly. My hands felt sticky on Beauty's stock. I left my friendly casaurina tree and worked around to the bottom of the yard. Still couldn't see anything to alarm me. There the yard was open between me and the house, so I went back to the casaurina tree and crossed toward the house under cover of some hibiscus bushes. The lights were on inside and I could just barely make out two voices speaking. Jedson was supposed to be traveling alone so far as I had been able to find out. A visitor? A bodyguard? A secretary? He'd had two bodyguards at the retreat on Saturday, probably them. His official vehicle was the only one parked on the street in front. I crawled directly under the nearest window and started to stand up in hopes of overhearing what was being said, at least enough to learn if it was a visitor who might leave if I waited awhile.

What sort of alarm it was I set off, I have no idea. I didn't hang around to ask. All I know is that it made a horrendous racket, someone shouted, "Down!" and someone else started shouting orders in Spanish. Lots of noise and someone burst out the back-door at the same moment the front door was flung violently open. I left—fast.

I could have holed up somewhere and waited, with quite good

chances of not being found, but sooner or later the Landrover would be noticed and searched. The plastic explosive and the fake license plate would give things away pretty quick and it would be impounded or some such. I didn't want to lose it, so I decided to get clear of the area entirely. I could hear someone running not far behind me. If I could hear him, he'd most likely heard me too, so I quit worrying about concealment and ran for the Landrover flat out. Didn't waste time zigzagging, etc., hoping he wouldn't shoot in such a crowded residential area. Jedson wouldn't be too popular if one of his minions shot some local woman or child. Must be bodyguards—Cuban ones from the sound of it. Cuba is about the only country that manages to make Spanish sound guttural. Whoever was shouting back there certainly didn't sound Belizean. There is some Spanish spoken in Belize but it doesn't sound like that.

I leaped the drain, skidded around the front of the Landrover, nearly yanked the door off its hinges and got out of there. Within half a mile I could see lights coming up fast in the rearview mirror. I thanked whatever gods may be that I had the Landrover I did rather than the rental one. No Landrover is built for speed though some can touch 80 or even 90 m.p.h. Most are straining by 70. That rental one, with its solid metal top, is topheavy and unstable at any sort of speed. This one, with a short wheelbase and light-weight canvas top, was virtually impossible to roll, and much faster. I put my foot flat on the floor and prayed no one was walking in the middle of the street. (One person was, but had excellent reflexes.)

I grabbed a quick look in the rearview mirror. Looked like a sedan of some sort behind me. Whatever, it was gaining fast on the paved road out of Belmopan. It also started throwing lead in my direction. I hunched lower in the seat and was glad Landrover seats are metal backed. Not very thick metal, but better than nothing. The outside rearview mirror shattered, but so far as I know that was the only bullet that hit anything. I didn't slow up for the Tee junction with the Hummingbird Highway, just yanked the wheel left ahead of the junction and went into it broadside. The car nearly took out the bus shelter on the opposite side.

Once we were heading south into the mountains on a narrow, twisting road full of huge potholes, the sedan started falling behind. That road gives unsuspecting tourists heart failure even in daylight. Badly washed-out areas alternate with loose gravel and blind curves. I've driven it many times and know the worst holes and curves by heart. The people in the other car obviously didn't. They stopped shooting—probably too busy hanging on for dear life. I had a little time to consider what to do.

First: who were they? They were with Jedson and obviously expecting trouble. Someone had set up an electronic alarm system of some sort, and their car had been parked away from Jedson's house. Accent sounded Cuban. Their weapons sounded like Soviet AKMs, though I wouldn't stake my life on it. I was fairly sure there weren't more than a half dozen of them, difficult for Jedson to have brought any more anyway. I had the feeling they'd come straight after me without searching for anyone else. They would surely have left a minimum of two to guard Jedson and there was at least one driving and one shooting. The way the car was wallowing around on the road behind me made me think there were probably four or five people in it. Had they been expecting me? Seemed likely. This looked like a reception committee arranged for me personally. I would have to work on the assumption that these were the people who'd tried to kill me on the mountain, unlikely as that seemed—they'd tried to kill me before I'd even *heard* of Jedson! Didn't make sense. But if they weren't expecting me, they were certainly expecting someone. Why here?

I could lose them on the Hummingbird Highway, just gain a couple of miles, trade Landrovers and drive right past them in the other direction in the rental one. But then what? Even if I could get back and take out Jedson and his guards before they realized they'd lost me and returned, I wouldn't be able to hang around to get them too. As soon as a shot was fired at Jedson's house, people would be calling the cops, the army, and God knows who else. I hadn't seen their car well enough to be sure of identifying it again either. That would leave me still not knowing who had broken my cover and with several of whoever probably had, still out to kill me. No thanks.

Ideally I'd take out the car behind me first, then Jedson and his guards. But I wanted some time with one of them still alive and able to talk. I had to know who they were and who knew my identity.

That complicated matters. A "road accident" would probably kill all of them at the speeds we were going. 'Course, if they blew another corner as bad as that last one they might settle the debate for me. Wouldn't be much left of them to question though if they went off along here.

Then I was very busy with a patch of gravel I didn't see in time. Spun a full circle and glanced off the mud embankment. By the time the tires caught and I was pointing in the right direction again, their lights were practically touching my bumper. One glance at the remaining rearview mirror showed someone trying to lean a gun out the window at me. But they'd hit the same gravel I had and they were very busy too. The gun vanished.

I grinned into the night and put my foot down. But I had to decide what to do soon. Once the hills leveled out, they'd catch me easily and I didn't get the feeling they wanted me alive. When I'd gained enough of a lead again to be able to think, the plan that had been struggling to form itself in the back of my mind succeeded and I knew what I was going to do, or try to do anyway. About five miles ahead, the hills opened out briefly into the Cave's

Branch River Valley before closing in again. That was where the Hummingbird Lumber Company was based. Their sawmill was right beside the road. I didn't want to play tag in there, not with as many as I thought were in that car. But Cave's Branch Valley is full of caves and one cave, Mountain Cow Cave, was only twenty minutes walk from the sawmill. It is a beautiful cave that I had been to many times. A cave with two entrances. A big one the path leads to. If you didn't stop to look at anything you could go through the main rooms in 45 minutes if you knew the cave and hurried.

Then there was the zigzag at the end. The time I went down it, we took an hour each way. I thought I could remember it, though, so I shouldn't waste time taking wrong turns, etc. Say half an hour. . . . No one had ever actually gone out the other entrance as it was too small to get through, but it had looked like an easy job to enlarge it sufficiently.

They couldn't afford to leave their car unprotected so one man would be left with it. The man I was going to talk to—if it all worked right. The others would follow me. Hopefully, anyway. They wouldn't know whether there was another entrance or not, so presumably most would go in after me. They'd probably leave at least one man on guard at the mouth. Bobby's explosives would come in handy after all. That plastic could take care of the ones who came in after me. I'd leave a little present for them just inside the first narrow spot. With luck the one or ones on guard outside would stay there. They'd have no way of knowing who was alive and who wasn't. They would most likely have been ordered to wait for a certain length of time before going for reinforcements. If so, I should be out of the back entrance and waiting for them at the car.

Meant leaving more to chance than I like, but still seemed better than breaking contact with them and giving them time to call in additional personnel. Conceivably, they might even talk Jedson into leaving the country. Then he'd have half the Cuban Army to protect him if he wanted.

I climbed on the brakes at the top of the hill before Cave's Branch. A tight double curve down a steep hill ended in a long narrow bridge. A lot of accidents have happened there. I almost added another one to the list. My brakes were already doing about all they could before I saw the little Mini on the bridge. Fortunately Minis and Forces Landrovers are both narrow vehicles. Then mine was a touch narrower after I skimmed the railing and flattened one side a bit—sounded horrendous but the Landrover was still going like a bat out of hell when we got off the other end so apparently I hadn't damaged anything too critical. That bridge was meant for one car at a time. What happened to the Mini, I don't know, but as I spun into the sawmill I saw the sedan coming over my end of the bridge still in one piece. I stopped as far back in the mill yard as I could get.

Shoved the plastic and the flashlight into my shirt, grabbed Beauty and ran. Piles of old reject lumber and sawdust and low brush. Reached the beginning of the path just as they screeched to a halt beside the Landrover. I waited out of sight for a second to make sure they'd seen where I'd gone. Shouted orders and running boots—they'd seen me. I bolted off down the path. Once we were into the brush proper, I had to use my flashlight much of the time. I knew where the path went but if I got off it, easy to do in the dark, I'd waste time I couldn't afford finding it again. Over the saddle, through a dip and where the path looks like it turns left, you go right for Mt. Cow Cave. I could hear them crashing along behind me. Made sure I made plenty of noise starting up the hill so they wouldn't follow the path to the left too far. Didn't want to lose them yet. That hill is steep. I've never run up it before. I was gasping and totally drenched with sweat by the time I came to the natural amphitheater in front of the cave. I hoped the men behind me were worse off than I was. Or at least as badly out of breath.

I shone the flashlight over the edge. Wet leaves reached up. Below them the ground sloped steeply. I wouldn't have swung over that first drop into the entrance so rapidly without a rope, and on wet rocks, if I hadn't gone down it numerous times before. I knew it wasn't as bad as it looked, but I hoped it would slow down the men behind me. They wouldn't know where the footholds were and would waste time looking. They would take longer coming down the loose rubble slope, too. I'd cut it pretty fine between making sure they would see where I had gone to earth—literally— and allowing myself time to set up the booby trap I was counting on.

There is only one small hole leading out of the rubble-filled entrance room into the rest of the cave. You lean out over a black hold, brace yourself on a stalactite, then let go and drop. Before I did so, I shoved the wad of plastic under a projecting bit of rock, blessing Bobby for making me bring the stuff along—and the impulse that made me leave it in the Landrover instead of the pack. Gingerly, I inserted a detonator and unreeled the wire, running it down a crack as far as possible, then rubbing mud over it for the few inches I couldn't hide. I hoped it wouldn't be noticed but their lights seemed brighter than my flashlight.

No more time. I could hear them on the rubble slope close by now. I went over fast and flipped the wire as high as I could to the right. Missed. Could see their lights now. Tried again. And again. I was sweating blood before I finally got it behind a formation that would keep the damn thing up high and out of sight. I flung first the reel and then myself over the next ledge. Some idiot fired behind me and bullets ricocheted everywhere. The noise was deafening. Someone cursed vigorously in Spanish and they didn't fire again, to my considerable relief. They didn't like the ricochets any better than I did.

I felt for the reel of wire. In my dive for shelter, I'd smashed my shoulder on a rock and clipped myself on the chin with my rifle. I had no idea where my flashlight was.

Please, not in the entrance above me! I hoped to god I could fasten the switch to the wire in the dark. Christ! My hands were solid mud. Frantically, I wiped them on my shirt and rubbed off the connections as best I could. Feeling in the dark, I screwed the wires down tightly, hoping there wasn't so much mud on them that they wouldn't work. My chances of seeing daybreak weren't very good if they didn't.

I flipped the switch and the world went up. The rock I was on bucked and heaved like a raft in rough water. The noise was beyond anything I'd ever experienced before. More pressure than noise. Even a tank exploding beside you isn't that bad! At least the noise has somewhere to go above ground. Bits of rock and mud rained on me. Then something heavy smashed across my back, sheathing it in pain. Eventually, the noise subsided except for isolated crashes as parts of the roof and walls continued falling.

I never have liked plastic explosives and don't know that much about them despite all Bobby's efforts to teach me. If I think I'm going to need explosives on a job, I take an expert with me. I never thought about the confining effect of the cave. Probably used six times what I needed to. Likely sealed my own fate, as well, by doing so.

I hurt everywhere. I had no light and was pinned under something terribly heavy. Even if I did get out from under whatever it was, and by some miracle found my flashlight, and by another miracle it still worked, I'd be very lucky if most of the rest of the cave hadn't collapsed as well.

My mind started to run away with itself. Trapped in blackness. All the secret nightmares no caver ever dares admit leaped and danced on my terror. I forced the panic back. First things first. Rolled Beauty out from under my shoulder and throat. Braced my hands and tried to heave the weight off my back. It shifted slightly. Shoulders aching and arms trembling, I strained over and over again, gaining a little more purchase each time. One final heave and the weight slid to one side, taking what felt like half my back with it.

I was free! Control the first impulse to bolt. Lie still. Think. Wait for the dizziness to pass. Try to think how I was oriented before the blast. I talked to myself like I was a frightened moron—wasn't far off just then, either.

Start by feeling everywhere I can without moving from where I am. No flashlight. Lay the rifle beside the rock I was under so I can find it again. Move to the left and start again. And again. This time my hand gropes over space. Can't touch bottom. Back up to where I estimate I started from and begin the process to the right. That way ends in a wall. Move forward and work my way back to the edge again. Forward once more, and this time I can feel a wall ahead of me as well. The one I dived over? If so, I'm still fairly well oriented. Then I've searched all the flat area ahead of me. I crawled back to the rock that had landed on me and felt along it on both sides. No flashlight, though I found the wire reel. Can't see any use for it now but I put it beside my rifle, so I can find it again and go on searching methodically. Then, I cracked my head painfully on a rock sticking out from the wall, just missing my eye. More carefully, now, feeling ahead at face level as well. Eventually, I've felt over the perch I'm on entirely. Walls along two sides and a dropoff in front.

Back to where I think I dove over earlier. If I could climb up just a few feet I should be able to pull myself up onto the ledge above. Then I discovered that balance relies on sight to a great extent. I fell back down several times before realizing that there was no ledge anymore. Just more rock. Apparently that whole section of passage had collapsed. If my flashlight was under there, it was going to stay there for the rest of time. I wasn't going anywhere either if that was the case. It took much longer to control the panic this time.

Well, I was certainly going to die if I stayed on my ledge. Started feeling sorry for myself.

Still, I don't die easy or I'd be dead a hundred times over by now. Probably would be soon but I wasn't yet. I'd done all I could from where I was and I couldn't go up, so that only left down. I had no idea how far a drop it might be. Still, if it was a long one, it made for a quicker death than starving here. And it might be only a little farther than I could reach. Estimated as best I could where my flashlight would have gone over, assuming it had, then I slid the rifle over the edge. Sounded like it stopped fairly soon. Trying not to think about broken bones, I lowered myself over the edge till I was hanging by my hands.

I dropped, twisting so that if there were any rocks sticking out I'd catch them on my hip and shoulder instead of in the gut or on the chin. Acquired a few more bruises and caught a rock in the gut anyway, but I didn't fall very far. I gagged and choked trying to get air back into my lungs.

When I could breathe again I sat up. My foot hit something that clinked. Must just be a rock. I grabbed for it. A thousand-to-one-chance—covered in mud but unmistakably a flashlight. With every ounce of my being I willed it to go on as I pushed the switch. Nothing. Told myself that really had been too much to hope for. There was still a chance. There was just room in the cap in this style to tape a spare bulb. I was often in situations where I couldn't afford to be suddenly without lights because of a broken bulb, so I always carry a spare.

Started to unscrew the cap frantically. Whoa. Wait. Easy does it. I carefully took off my shirt and spread it over my lap. Now I couldn't lose any pieces. Next, wipe my hands as free of mud as I can on the inside of my sleeves. *Now* unscrew the cap and feel for the spare bulb. Screw the cap back on, so I won't drop the batteries out as I unscrew the other end. Three pieces. Lens and outer casing. Reflector and bulb. Got the spare bulb in and the reflector back in place and screwed the whole lot back together again. I had never realized how complicated flashlights are until I tried to assemble one in total darkness with my life depending on the results.

I was almost afraid to try the switch. When I did, nothing happened. Nothing. I pushed the switch on and off, over and over. Nothing. There is no blackness deeper than that which I sat in. To have actually found the flashlight and to have a spare bulb as well and still be sentenced to die here slowly, by inches, was too much to take. I wondered how long it would be before I went mad. Not very long if the way I felt now was any guide. I had to do something, anything to hold onto my sanity. There was nothing else to do, so I took the flashlight apart and cleaned it as best I could by feel and reassembled it. I must have done that half a dozen times when suddenly it came on.

There is simply no way to describe my feelings. That sort of last-minute reprieve is hard on the heart. I must have simply sat there staring at it a full minute before it occurred to me to do anything else. That faint beam of light was the most beautiful thing in creation. I looked at it in awe.

Then everything that had led up to this faint beam of light came back with a rush. There were still people who would kill me given the chance. Had they all been killed by the explosion? I wondered briefly if any of them was perhaps caught as I had been, trapped with no light. But I didn't waste much sympathy, I'm afraid. That was their problem, not mine. Besides, if they hadn't been trying to kill me they wouldn't have been there. What did matter to me, though, was whether they'd left anyone on guard outside the cave entrance and, if so, how long he would stay there. They almost certainly would have left someone. Too much chance of my hiding on one side of the rubble slope while they came down the other and either getting the drop on them or sneaking back out unseen. But what would he do after the lower entrance blew up? How well disciplined was he? Would he call it a day and get out of there as fast as possible? In which case I'd gained nothing. Once the survivors got in their car and left, I had no good way of finding them before they could get reinforcements. I had to get one of them alone for a while and ask him a few questions.

I had to get out of there first. I blessed the heavy durable flashlight and its longlasting batteries. I flashed the light around and couldn't recognize a thing. The lovely series of short passage-ways draped with beautiful crystal were gone completely. Raw jagged rock thrust up all around and I was standing in mud and debris in a crevasse between two huge slabs of muddy rock. I put my shirt back on, found my rifle and started down the crevasse I was in. Heading, I hoped, roughly in the direction the passage used to take.

I spent what felt like hours climbing over rocks and crawling through gaps. A landslide above ground is awesome. Under-ground, it is simply terrifying. I swore that if I ever got out of this elemental hell, I was never going into a cave again.

I crawled down one more slab and into the opening below and suddenly realized the mud under my hands was smooth and hard-packed. I crept forward on hands and knees and flashed my light around. Definitely undisturbed mud. The contours of it looked like the mud passage between the first rooms and the Breakdown Room. But the ceiling hadn't been so low before. You had to crouch down in a couple of places but you didn't have to actually crawl. Still, I was pretty sure I knew where I was. Surely I must have come farther than that? Of course I might well have gone around in circles a bit in that mess I'd just come through. I was so glad to be out of it I could have cried. Another 20 feet and I knew for sure. There was an abrupt rise in the floor with steps worn in it. Where I could walk up before, there wasn't room to crawl through now. But the shock that had lowered the ceiling had loosened it as well and I was able to dig away enough to squirm through in short order. I wondered how long it had been since the explosion. The longer I took to get out, the slimmer my chances were if I did. No idea. My watch had shattered during the explosion and was useless.

Fifty feet more and the ceiling rose in the entrance to the Breakdown Room. The scramble up seemed virtually unchanged. My hopes soared as I flashed my light up the first slope and saw the flowstone stalagmite I always used for a marker still growing up from the rock beside me. Apparently the destruction hadn't reached here. I supposed I had the mud passage to thank for that. It was much smaller and set at a lower level than the rooms I'd been in when I set off the explosion. Most of the force of the blast must have been contained in those rooms. It was severe enough there to drop the ceiling of the mud passage, but that in itself had probably helped to keep the rest of the cave undamaged.

The Breakdown Room is enormous. Centuries ago the roof caved in. The result is a tremendous pile of jumbled rocks stretching from one side of the room nearly to the other. It happened so long ago that huge flowstone pillars have formed on top of this former ceiling. Even small stalagmites take hundreds of years to form. Many of these are 20 to 30 feet high. They don't come anywhere near the roof. When it first happened it must have looked much like the devastation behind me.

The ancient Mayans had used caves in Belize to collect pure "holy" water that dripped from the stalactites hanging from the cave roofs. I'd seen ancient burial sites in other caves. Flowstone-covered skeletons. And there had been pottery shards in the front rooms of this cave before I blew it up. Cama Zotz, the Bat God, ruled the Mayan underworlds. With a flaming tongue, a single huge claw on the end of each arm and white "death eyes" on black wings, Cama Zotz seemed an appropriate demon god to preside over the chaos behind me.

As I came to the top of the mound, I saw that the Breakdown Room hadn't escaped damage entirely. There used to be a group of tall crystalline columns at the highest point in the room that you climbed up and through. Now they were lying broken in a treacherous-looking tangle. I skirted around them carefully and started the descent on the other side of the room. Soon, I could see the top of the huge column that guides one down, a perfect symmetrical shining-white column, 30 feet high with a domed top. Yet the room it's in dwarfs it. I didn't stop to admire it this time, but scrambled down off the loose rocks and headed toward the grotto beyond.

You squeeze through a tiny gap in a seemingly solid wall of formations and find yourself completely inside a single crystalline formation. Slender crystal draperies ring with clear echoing notes if they're tapped.

I hauled myself up and was met by solid rock. A section of flowstone had come loose from the roof and now filled the gap into the grotto completely. It must have weighed several tons. I dropped back down.

There is another way into the back rooms if I could remember where. I'd looked through a "window" once years ago back into

the Breakdown Room. I closed my eyes and tried to picture what
I had seen from the ''window'' that day. That's right. I'd thought
I'd discovered a new room until I realized there couldn't be two
such huge perfectly symmetrical columns in the same cave. In my
mind's eye, I could see the back side of it and below me was a
smooth steep flowstone waterfall. Must be farther along this same
wall. I crossed to the back of the huge column and shone my light
along the wall. There was a bit of an alcove directly across from
me. The back of it rose in an unbroken sheet of crystal flowstone.
That was the only spot that looked at all like what I remembered,
so I went over. Couldn't see any opening in it, but maybe I would
when I got up it. If I got up it. It looked awfully smooth and the
angle was damn near perpendicular. On closer inspection, the
surface was furrowed with tiny ridges which would give good
friction. I definitely needed both hands free for this. I could shove
my flashlight in my waistband. It would hurt my balance there and
probably shine in my eyes more than on the rock, but it would
have to do. How on earth was I going to get my rifle up there even
if I could get myself up?

Leave the rifle and see if I was even in the right spot first. Then
worry about it. To my relief the climb proved quite easy and
shorter than it looked. Best of all the ''window'' was there. I sat
in it and dangled my legs over while I considered the situation.
Then I wedged the flashlight where it would provide light for me
while I climbed down. Took off my shirt and tied one sleeve
around the barrel and the other through the trigger guard. Instant
sling. Stuck my head and one arm through and climbed back up.
Untied Beauty, caught my breath and put my shirt on again.

Now, where was I? Figured I should have bypassed the grotto
and been somewhere near the flowstone Mobius Strip Room. That
room was well named. Anyone setting off to circle it would come
back to where they started from all right, but the marker arrow

would be pointing the opposite direction to what it should be. I set off in the general direction I thought the Mobius Strip should be, and soon things began to look familiar.

I was worn out and lugging a rifle. The relief of having the flashlight work and still being alive had began to wear off. The cave seemed interminable. I hurt in so many places. And I was so tired. It hadn't been that long since I fled from Belmopan but getting that rock off my back, and the subsequent tension and getting out of the caved-in area had drained me completely. Putting one foot in front of another was an effort, let alone having to worry about falling and breaking my neck.

Several times I wasted rapidly-dwindling time and energy by going down the wrong turning. Lost all idea of time. Existence blurred into endless passageways. Found myself heading back the way I'd come a couple of times.

Gradually the smell of wet leaves permeated the air and I could feel a bit of a breeze. I followed it until the passage ended. I knew the opening was high up on the right. When I'd done this route before, I'd thought about the possibility of trying to enlarge the opening but decided not to bother. I hoped I'd been right, that it could be enlarged. If not, I was going to have a whole cave for a tombstone. I left the rifle at the bottom and climbed up. All I had besides my hands was my Spanish dagger. Not the tool I would have chosen for digging. I was afraid I'd snap the blade, but those Spaniards knew how to make good steel. The blade didn't break, even when I used it to pry out loose pieces of rock. When the hole was just barely big enough to let me squeeze through, I went back for my rifle.

Wet leaves against my face. Fresh air. Rain. I was back in the living world again.

I sat up and tried to work out where I was while I cleaned the worst of the mud off Beauty. Tried to picture Mountain Cow Cave as a 3-D map in my mind. As best I could work out, I should be on the side of the hill facing toward the highway, between a third and halfway around it from the main entrance. There would be a hill between me and the sawmill. All I could see was jungle shadows. But I didn't know if I was right. I might be a lot closer to the main entrance than I thought. Decided not to risk the flashlight until I got to the bottom of the hill. Put it in my shirt and put my knife back in its sheath. Walking in jungle at night without a path to follow is stupid: without a light is worse. Everything has thorns. Some are several inches long, the diameter of sewing needles.

I stepped over a ledge in the dark, grabbed out instinctively and got a handful of thorns. Fell about ten feet, landing with a jolt that left my right leg numb. Spent the next five minutes picking out as many thorns as I could by flashlight. A lot had broken off under the skin. My hand hurt. I decided to risk using the flashlight after all.

Finally, I stepped out onto the Hummingbird Highway. I hadn't crossed Cave's Branch River and couldn't see the sawmill; therefore, I must be south of the mill somewhere, and I turned left and walked up the road. No doubt I should have run, now that I was back where I could. Missing them by a few minutes would be just as bad as missing them by a few hours. I walked. I'd reached that state of exhaustion where you simply don't care. One foot in front of the other, okay, but run? No way!

I put the flashlight away as soon as I hit the road. Plenty of moonlight once I was out of the bush. Too much. Once I got past the first building I got off the road. Soon I could see the back of the yard. The Landrover and the sedan were still there. Maybe I hadn't used up all my luck. All of a sudden I felt alive again.

I circled around and came in from the north side through the mill itself. It is a long open building, roofed-over but no walls. The saws and conveyer belt run in a line down the center. There were stacks of boards leaning criss-crossed on drying racks in front, and the office building to the left. The sedan was just past the main office. There should've been a night watchman but I didn't expect to see him. Someone from the sedan would have disposed of him. (I hoped not fatally.)

I crawled on my hands and knees down the north side of the conveyor belt. Then on my belly in between the lumber stacks. There I could stand up. I peered between two boards, breathing in the rich smell of new lumber. I could see a guard leaning against the building closest to the sedan with his back partly turned toward me. Not very well-trained from the looks of it—his gun was propped against the wall in front of him and he had his hands in his pockets.

For the second time in a week I made a cosh out of my sock. No sudden rush this time, though. Not with a man trained, however poorly, in the art of killing. Not when he had a gun within reach. I would take a couple of seconds to reach him and if his hearing was good, and he was decently trained, that would be time enough for him to shoot me. So I left my boots off and sneaked up on him one cautious step at a time, not touching my heels to the ground. Feeling with each foot carefully, and only putting my weight on it gradually when I was sure there was nothing that would make noise under it. I only tapped him gently—I was going to want him conscious soon.

I opened the sedan driver's side door and dragged him over to it. Heaved and shoved him into the seat. Strapped him in with the shoulder-style seat belts. He looked okay except his head lolled. I got his belt off and strapped his legs together with it. Found a rag under the seat that made an effective gag. Then I tied one end of it to the shoulder strap as high up as I could and that stopped his head flopping over. The angle could have been better but from a distance he should pass. Nothing to tie his hands with so I cut off his sleeves, tied them together and then tied his hands to the lapstrap so he couldn't raise them. Shut the door and retreated to my spot behind the stack of boards. Nothing to do now but put my boots and socks back on and wait.

The rain stopped. The moonlight shone brighter yet. The mosquitos made sure I wasn't tempted to doze off. The man in the car recovered before the others returned. I could see him trying to twist his head. I began to wonder if they had all been killed in the explosion. Wished I knew how long it had been. Should've checked to see if the guard had a watch but I didn't think of it at the time, and I didn't want to leave my hide again. Was that just a firefly flashing over there? Gone. I kept watching. There it was again. No—maybe? Straining to see in the night. Concentrating totally on the tiny light in the distance. My heart nearly jumped out of my mouth when a rain-sodden board shifted in the stack behind me. I wonder how many fellow operators die of heart failure from things like that.

I looked again. Definitely a man with a headlamp. Then I could see a second man as well, also wearing a headlamp. I waited until they were well out in the open area in front of the vehicles before I opened fire, aiming an inch below the headlamps. If the headlamp was at hairline level, that would put the bullet in the middle of the forehead—if the headlamp was centered, the bullet would strike between the eyes. One head lamp went out immediately, the other fell to the ground, shining up into the trees. No sounds or signs of movement, so after a moment I went over to the sedan and switched on the headlights. They shone on two crumpled bodies but I approached cautiously, outside of the cone of light provided by the sedan, just in case one of them was faking. They weren't. One had half his head blown off. The other was missing his throat and most of his shoulder. The explosion and being dragged through the cave didn't seem to have done Beauty any harm. I walked back to the car.

I undid the seat belt and motioned my captive out. He didn't move so I raked Beauty across his face and yanked him out. Backed the Landrover over beside him and motioned him to stand up and get in the door I held open. He could manage that even with his legs tied together, since his hands were tied in front. I wasn't about to risk undoing his legs. A well aimed blow from a boot can kill as well as one from a hand—maybe even easier. Once he was seated, I clipped him lightly over the ear with Beauty's butt and caught him as he sagged. He was only out for a couple of minutes but it gave me time to do up the seat belt and tie his hands to it. Not a shoulder-type harness in my Landrover but it would keep him in his seat. I didn't want him suddenly lunging at me as we were going around a corner. Knocking him out again might have been unnecessary, but I knew a man who got killed because he thought a tied prisoner was helpless. The guy's hands were tied all right—he used them together like a sledge hammer on the back of the operator's neck and broke it.

I closed the door and went around to my side. Drove out of the yard turning north. I knew where I would take my captive. There was an abandoned gravel pit that was quite extensive a few miles farther back the way we'd come. I could drive in nearly an eighth of a mile there, out of sight of the highway, and out of earshot as well.

The road was deserted all the way to the gravel pit. I turned and drove right to the back. The bush loomed just ahead in a solid wall. The moon was starting to wane. I turned off the engine and looked at my captive. I knew what had to be done. I thought of the other times. Of how utterly sickening and soul-debasing torture was. It would have to be the knife. It was all I had to use. A man used a knife on me once. I did not want to torture this man. Neither did I want to die. Before it had been other people's lives that had been at stake. This time it was my own. That made it worse in a way. Torture, unlike killing, does not become easier. Or if it ever does. . . .

I got out and went around to his side, opened the door and dragged him out. Something about his face pulled at my mind. I shone my flashlight on him, then removed the gag so I could see all of his face. Definitely recognized it from somewhere. Flipped through my mental file of dossiers. Got him. Guiterra, something Guiterra. Political appointee in Havana's secret police. Rumored to be the boyfriend of their top man. A political appointee who had never been field-trained, with a reputation for conducting interrogations in person and continuing them long after they had served any use. Some of my sick feeling went. I knew it didn't make what I was about to do any better, but I couldn't help but feel that if I was going to torture someone, I would rather him than most.

He would know more than I had dared hope. Far from being the guard ordered to stay behind, he must be the one who gave the orders and had chosen the "safe" job for himself, sending his men out into the jungle to hunt me.

He started to speak but I retied the gag cutting him off and said in Spanish: "Guiterra, you are a long way from your desk in Havana. Or from your interrogation rooms. There are things I wish to know that you will tell me. When you have decided to speak nod your head and I will remove the cloth."

He looked stunned at my knowledge of his name, nationality and occupation. Bobby had taught me well. I gave him no time to think over what I knew, and infer from that what all I might not know. Starting out mildly and building up pain slowly gives the victim time to prepare what mental resources he can. I drew my knife, gripped his left eyelid and cut it away. Pain from a wound that cannot be seen and that is close to a vital organ is far more persuasive than pain from one that can be seen not to be serious. One's own blood blinding one has its own particular horror too.

Some people are screamers. Some aren't. He was a screamer. Guiterra hadn't been trained to resist torture. Time stretches unrecognizably at such times but in real time it didn't take very long. When I finished I thought over everything I'd learned while I wiped my knife clean on the gag. Was there anything more he could tell me? Then I realized cleaning my knife had been a wasted effort. I didn't want to risk a gunshot here. They carry farther than screams do. His had been muffled by the gag most of the time anyway. I finished the job and cleaned my knife again. My thoughts echoed in the sudden silence. Gradually, the bush sounds filled the night again.

I sat there longer than I should have. The night wouldn't last forever and I still had three men to kill and a Landrover to dispose of before daybreak. I left his body where it was and got back into the Landrover, driving towards Belmopan once again. No pre-job tenseness this time. I felt utterly exhausted in body and soul both, like I'd lived about a hundred years too long. I made myself review what he'd told me.

There was a rather complicated little dust-up in Colombia a couple of months ago that I had been involved in. By the end of it, there were agents from half a dozen countries besides Colombia involved. Cuba was one, as always if there's trouble in Latin America. One of Guiterra's men was there checking up on another Cuban agent who was suspected of being a traitor. It was sheer bad luck that he ever saw me. Worse luck that he had a good memory for faces and was in the Bogota Airport when I left. He promptly changed his plans and tailed me instead, losing me when I went to Headquarters but picking me up again after I left. Fortunately I hadn't gone home, that time, but straight to the climbing club.

There was a climb planned for that weekend before I ever left for Colombia. I just barely had time to catch the other climbers if

I didn't take time to go home first. So, Guiterra's man followed me to the climbing club and joined the club himself. He came along several weekends. I had vanished into thin air as far as he knew, but by that time he knew Paul was my partner so he struck up with him. Pumped him as much as he could. Paul knew I had family in Belize. Of such small things is an operator's grave dug. Paul also knew I was seldom gone for more than a few weeks. So the man had waited, and tried to kill me, though he was not an assassin. When that failed, he reported back to Guiterra who was in Belize by then. Guiterra pulled him out and ordered him to Belize also. My hide was saved by Guiterra's conceit. He never passed the information about me on to any higher-ups because he didn't want to admit the failed murder attempt on the mountain— didn't want to admit his man had gotten Paul instead of me.

Guiterra had a man posted at the Belize airport to watch for any known CIA agent. They were halfway expecting an attempt on Jedson's life. Guiterra briefed the man to watch for me as well. When I arrived they made no effort to keep a tail on me as such. Guiterra knew I knew Belize better than they did, so they concentrated on protecting Jedson. Figured they'd kill me when I came for him. The man who recognized me was one of those I'd just killed. The only others who knew anything about me were the two men still guarding Jedson in Belmopan. I would have to be certain I killed both of them as well.

I left the Landrover a mile down the highway from the Belmopan turnoff. Didn't want to be seen either, not covered in cave mud and blood. The rain had washed a lot of the mess off but I was definitely not fit to be seen, too likely to draw attention. Started hiking. I had recovered a lot during the drive back. Wouldn't say I felt exactly fresh, but I wasn't completely dead anymore either.

A lone pair of headlights came along as I was walking down

the approach to Belmopan. I dropped flat in the grass. They passed and I went on. I wanted to get into the monsoon drains as soon as I could. Tried to remember how they ran. As you approach the town you meet the government buildings and the marketplace first. Then there is a long open area leading up the slope toward the residential areas. Three concrete paths lead up to the housing areas. I was pretty sure there was a drain along the nearer one of them. I risked a dash across the road and a stretch of grass and nearly fell into it. I thought it was the far side of the path—it wasn't. And, of course, it had been raining for several hours. I made good time despite wading upstream. Regiments of mosquitos flew escort.

Luck was with me and my drain led to the right section of town. Then I noticed the telephone line. It was slung from the electricity poles, several feet below the power lines. Not too thick a cable so it must just be the phones in this section of town. Lovely. I left my drain under cover of some trees just long enough to cut it, sawing through the heavy copper wire with my much abused dagger. Back into the main drain and continued towards Jedson's house. Turned down the wrong connecting drain and cautiously stuck my head up right in front of a little dog which promptly started barking furiously. I beat a hasty retreat with the little dog following, raising the alarm at the top of its lungs all the way to the main drain. Anywhere but Belmopan or Belize City and I'd have had to kill it as fast as possible and pray no one came to investigate. Considering where I was, I just thought about killing it. Dogs bark all night, every night in Belmopan and no one pays attention to them. I've never understood having watchdogs (and all Belizean dogs are watchdogs at least in theory) when they bark over nothing so constantly that no one notices when it's for real, but tonight I was very glad.

Found the right connecting drain and checked out the situation from a safe distance. Cops' Landrover parked in front. Two cops very noticeably on duty in the front yard. I crawled out and sneaked up on the house from the opposite side to the way I had come earlier. Two more cops lounging on the back porch. Lights in the house. I wasn't overly concerned about the cops. Regular police aren't trained to cope with trained assassins. However, I did want to know where Jedson and his two guards were. One should be inside with Jedson and one outside, on the roof or in a tree where he could cover all approaches. Where?

I couldn't see much of the roof nor could I see into the trees very well. Couldn't see much of a damn thing, really. Didn't dare go any closer till I had the outside man located and, preferably, out of the way. So, back to the drain and around the block so as to come in from the side I had before. Crept up to the same casaurina tree I'd sheltered under earlier and hoped it wasn't the spot the guard had chosen for a lookout post. If so I was going to be very dead, very soon. Expecting a bullet in the spine any half-second, I crawled under its branches and slowly stood up. Couldn't see much but no one had shot me yet, so I climbed very slowly, careful not to shake the tree or break any of the brittle branches. No one. Beauty kept getting in my way. By the time I was eight feet up, I could see out and could see a lump on the roof line. I settled as comfortably as possible, hoping I'd picked a tree without too many ants, and waited. I wanted to know which way the man on the roof was facing.

Not that it was going to solve the problem. Even if I could get in without his seeing me, I'd never get out alive. If I shot him the noise would drastically cut down my chances of getting the other two. I considered throwing my knife but discarded that thought as well—even if my aim was good enough to kill him instantly, which was very unlikely at that distance, his body would almost certainly roll off the roof, alerting the others nearly as fast as a shot would.

The moon was almost gone and dawn would be coming soon. I couldn't wait much longer. I considered going back to the Landrover and making a Molotov Cocktail—I could get a bottle out of someone's trash on the way and there was gas and rags in the Landrover. I was deciding I'd have to break into someone's kitchen to get some matches when he sat up. Then he stood and stretched. Scratched himself, looked around, stretched again, then picked up his gun. The second I was sure he really was coming down, I started down myself. Could hardly believe my luck. They must be going to swap positions. I was out from under the tree as he climbed down onto a lattice wall at the end of the front porch. I crawled behind the same hibiscus bush I'd used before. But I stood up well away from the wall this time. If one of the cops in front stepped around the side for a piss just then, things were going to get difficult. As I looked in the window I could see through an open door into the next room.

The front door opened. Then I saw Jedson at the far end of the room. He was turning to face the man who came through the door. I sighted quickly and fired. Jedson's face shattered as I fired my second shot at the man in front of the door. He was a pro and already flinging himself flat. I thought I got him but before I could make sure cops were shooting at a lot of innocent bushes all over the place and I ran. Someone inside opened up as well. I don't believe they could have seen me but they could guess the most likely bushes. They started off with the two most likely points and in a couple of seconds had sprayed lead all along that side at roughly knee level. I ran, crouching behind the neighbors' bushes, out of their sight. Made it into the drain just before a solid sheet of lead passed over it. Landed face first in eight inches of muddy water. I crawled on hands and knees, holding Beauty out of the water, till I reached the crosswalk in front of the house beneath the street light.

Looked like all the cops had gone inside. I waited. I was glad

I'd cut the telephone cable. No one was phoning for any reinforcements. No neighbors were phoning the police station either. Someone was going to have to come out of that house—and they didn't know which door I was watching.

I began to realize I hadn't been quite fast enough. Felt like someone was drawing a hot ember across my shoulders and again six inches or so farther down. Felt around gingerly. What I could reach was just grazed. Calling things a bit close though. Some large insect crawled out of the water onto my thigh. I flicked it off. Weren't they ever going to make a move? What would I do if they didn't? I had to get the last two Cubans. With luck, the guard I'd shot at was dead or at least out of action, but I couldn't count on luck—I'd had my share of it for the night. So I had to assume he was still alive. But I couldn't stay here after dawn! To try to approach that house with so many of them inside would be suicide. They must have a cop at every window.

Or was someone even now creeping out the back door while I watched the front? I strained to hear any noise from the back of the house. Though what I expected to hear, with every dog in Belmopan still barking from all the gunfire, I don't know. My nerves stretched. I fought the desire to leave my position and check the back. I couldn't be in both places at once. Mosquitos whined around my ears and I slapped at them with wet hands.

The door flew open and five cops dashed for the police Landrover. But one stood out. Most young Belizean men have an easy loping run. Four did. One ran the way Bobby'd spent months training me to. I shot him. Twice to make certain. The other four jumped in their Landrover and took off. It wouldn't take them long to get to the station and come back with every cop in Belmopan. I wanted to be gone before then.

If one of the cops wasn't Belizean there must be another cop inside without a uniform, and one Cuban. Presumably the Cuban

I'd shot had swapped clothes with the remaining cop. I crawled down the drain the other way and climbed out again. Couldn't use the bushes I'd used before—there was hardly a leaf left on them after that hail of lead. The neighbor wasn't going to be very pleased—the bullets hadn't done the side of the house much good either. Tried to figure out where I would post two men to cover as many approaches as possible if I were inside Jedson's house. If there *were* only two. Wondered how far out that bloody electronic snooper field extended. There was a narrow angle behind the back corner of the house on my side that I didn't think they could see from anywhere inside.

I approached that way and stopped about three feet from the corner. Doubted the alarm's field extended that far but I wasn't taking any chances. Then someone inside got smart and turned off the lights. They should have as soon as I shot the first time, but I wished they hadn't. I waited. Silence. Pried a rock loose from a row edging a flower bed beside me. It was a cement block house with wood doors and glass louver windows. The windows would make so much noise I wouldn't be able to hear anything from inside, so I heaved the rock at the center of the door. A gun opened up and made a mess of the door. A Belizean accent yelled a frightened query from the north end of the house. A Cuban one shouted, "Stay there!" The one who shot the door. Would he come to investigate or stay where he was? Figured he'd stay put. He'd blasted the door right in the middle so he must be roughly in line with it. I turned and crept along the south wall, still keeping well out. Then I had to pass the window where the third man would be posted, if there was a third man.

Suddenly all the tensions of the last couple of months took their toll. I froze. I knew what was happening and I felt detached and calm but I could not make myself move. Crouched on the balls of my feet, frozen in place like someone playing the children's game, "Statues." But this was no game. Muscles began to ache. A mosquito whined in my ear and still I hung from my nerves, unable to move. Too many people had come too close to killing me in too short a space of time. My body mutinied. It flatly refused to step in front of that window and risk getting torn apart by bullets. I knew that the longer I stood there, the greater the risk was of someone seeing me, that I would never be safe again unless I succeeded in killing the last Cuban agent. The last one who knew what country I lived in and where I climbed. My body refused to listen. I coaxed it gently. Just once more and then you'll be safe again. Once more and there won't be any bears in the night that know where you are. One more, that's all. Another few minutes of risk and then you can be safe for as long as you need. Help me just a little longer. . . . Eventually, like a reluctant child, first one leg and then the other would bend again, muscles quivering as they relaxed sufficiently to function. Slowly, agonizingly slowly, I crept past the window. No bullets shattered my cringing body. Past three or four feet of cement wall. I stopped just below the corner of the south living room window.

He should be in the middle of the room somewhere. Finally there was a faint sound like someone shifting position slightly. Estimated where it was as closely as I could, slipped Beauty onto semi-automatic, leaning out in front of the window and firing as the barrel cleared the sill. Six shots at a vague blur then I dropped again instantly. All those hours practicing that move paid off once more. The return fire rained bits of glass and cement chips all over the yard but I was well down and nothing hit me. A light flashed and I could hear movement and a groan. Then footsteps coming into the room—the cop? Another groan as the footsteps drew closer. I must've hit the Cuban. I waited till I heard them whispering together then stood up very slowly till I could just barely see in. One on the floor and one bending over with a flashlight. The one on the floor saw me but not in time. I shot. Waited a split second as the cop jumped aside and shot the Cuban twice more to make absolutely sure. And ran. I wasn't interested in killing Belizean cops, only Cubans.

The cop fired off several rounds but I was already back in the drain, running down to the main monsoon drain. I was just starting down the slope beyond the houses when I heard something coming up the road fast. I sneaked a look and saw three police Landrovers overflowing with cops. They could clean up the mess. I wondered what they'd make of it—after all, Jedson was dead but no Belizean had even been hurt, yet there were a number of corpses around the country that might, or might not, be identified as Cuban. I would be curious to read the official version.

I got back to the Landrover without any mishaps. Turned her around and drove down the hill to the culvert where my pack was. Seemed like a century at least since I left it there. It was soaking. Hoped everything inside wasn't as well. False dawn lightened the sky. The moon was gone. The bullet grazes hurt too much to lean back against the seat as I drove slowly south past Cave's Branch, past the mill, past the Sibun River a couple of miles, to St. Margaret's Creek around a nasty sharp bend. There is a 30- or 40-foot drop-off just before the creek at the worst point in the curve. I stopped the Landrover and got out. Lifted out Beauty and the pack. Looked around inside to be sure I hadn't left anything, then wiped over everything I might've touched to remove any and all fingerprints.

Started the engine and inched her right to the edge, held the clutch down with my hand as I got out, let go of it and jumped back. I needn't have jumped. She took her time about moving but then went over with a certain dignity. A shame really, I'd grown quite fond of her. She'd done well by me.

Shouldered the pack, wincing, picked up Beauty and walked

slowly to the bridge. Dropped down beside it and waded up the creek. Lead weights pulled at my feet and my eyelids. My senses swam with pain. My flashlight startled a little bird asleep in a branch overhanging the creek. Shadow shapes loomed and leaped in the bushes. I'd hiked in this area before. Half a mile upstream was a sandy bank that should do, unless this year's rains had washed it away. It was still there, wider in fact than before. There would be no tracks leading away from the road into the bush since I'd walked in the stream. No earthly reason for anyone to come looking down here and this was well out of sight and sound of the road. Dropped the pack. Made a very poor attempt at shelter. Crawled into my sleeping bag with Beauty and passed out.

Chapter Five

AFTERMATH

PAUL SMILED a happy, friendly smile and slowly stuck a knife into my ear. When I asked him to remove it he shook his head, still smiling at me as he twisted it a bit deeper. I woke, swatting at the side of my head. My hand came away smeared with blood, a crushed black body with wings between my fingers. Deer fly.

Wiped it off and looked at the rest of my hand, wondering vaguely at the numerous scrapes. The whole heel of my palm was swollen and throbbing and I could just see a dozen or so tiny black dots in it. Then memory came back with a jolt. Those black dots were thorns, broken off under the skin when I fell off the ledge in the dark last night. After getting out of the cave. Before questioning Guiterra. Before killing Jedson. I was in a lean-to on St. Margaret's Creek. I hurt.

Tried to sit up to take stock. Someone was hammering railroad spikes between each section of my lower spine. I rolled onto my side and tried pushing myself up on my arm. Fire shot across my shoulders and my head swam. Shaking, sweat pouring off of me, I eased my arm back down, decided to take stock later, and passed out.

I woke again around noon, sweltering, with that revolting, drugged feeling that comes only from sleeping in the heat of the day in the tropics. Dying of thirst. Sat up very slowly and carefully. The pain didn't seem to have gone away any but the need for a drink overrode it. I literally crawled out of my shelter, over to the water, on hands and knees. My head was swimming so bad, I could barely see and I was shaking like the proverbial leaf. Lay face down and drank. Lay there for a long time letting the sun beat down on my back and the light breeze blow some of the cobwebs away.

But sun heat works miracles in aching bones and muscles. Eventually, I propped myself up and crawled out into the water where I wedged myself between a couple of rocks and let the water wash the worst off. It felt very cold on my sunheated body and the shock helped bring me around. I sat up slowly. Took off and attempted to wash out first my shirt, then my boots and socks and finally my pants. I could remember frightening a little bird while I was wading up the creek the night before but nothing after that. I looked around and saw I had made a half-assed shelter out of my mosquito net and flysheet. It was mostly collapsed and it didn't look like I'd bothered with a groundsheet, just dragged the sleeping bag in on the wet sand. My pack. There would be part of a bar of soap in there and a facecloth. Tried to stand up, then decided hands and knees were safer, not to mention less painful, for the moment.

Washing the mud and blood off, with the sunlight dancing on the water you didn't expect to be alive to see, is an inexpressible luxury. Best of all was the knowledge that there were no shadows that knew what mountains I roamed, that could follow me there. Lucy's "operator's-life-expectancy 50-50" just couldn't begin to compute the sheer glory of being alive. I hardly even minded the sea of pain that was my back and middle—if I could hurt that bad I had to be alive! For now that was enough.

Minnows fought over the scuzzy soap I rinsed off and bit at

my toes hoping for more. This time I stood and managed to stay upright as I went over to my pack and got out the solid fuel cooker and the coffee! Inspected the damage while the water heated. Nothing seemed broken but my entire stomach and back were badly bruised and swollen. Likely tendon and/or ligament damage to lower half of back. Also scraped raw by the rock when it shifted. Two bullet grazes across shoulders, gouges and bruises on legs and arms due to getting out of Mountain Cow Cave and stepping off the ledge. Plus the thorns in my hand which I proceeded to pick out with the sewing needle I'd borrowed from Sarah. To my surprise I also found another bullet graze on the side of my neck. No idea when I'd gotten it even. All in all I had been very, very lucky.

Dragged my sleeping bag out to dry in the sun and spread my clothes over some bushes to dry as well. Retreated with a mug of very strong, sweet coffee to a rock in the middle of the creek, to escape the bugs, and sat naked in the sun. I've gone alone into the hills wherever I've lived since I can remember; and the jungle doesn't try to harm you. If you come to grief it's your own fault. I've always found watching flowing water hypnotic and extremely relaxing. The pain killers I had taken when I got the coffee out were beginning to work.

Sunlight and water. A brilliant blue Morpho butterfly flew upstream past me. They wove through my day dreaming—wondering what I wanted out of this life that I was still rather surprised, but very grateful, to have.

I have no idea how long she'd been standing there looking at me before I saw her, but I gradually grew aware of another presence. Raised just my eyes to see a Brocket deer standing in the middle of the creek watching me. Brockets are small deer that look more like African Duikers than true deer. They have lovely rich reddish coats and huge ears and eyes. This one was a doe. The sun shone on her back and the light sparkled and glinted off the water swirling around her legs. A large branch hung out over the water between us, framing the scene. Ears outstretched, she took one slow step at a time toward me till she was so close I could see her nostrils quivering and wrinkling the velvet top of her nose. She stopped, frozen for a moment. Then she lowered her head to drink, still watching me, and slowly turned, disappearing into the bush on the other side of the creek.

Suddenly realized I'd been holding my breath the whole time. Somehow it was immensely comforting to think of such shy, gentle animals being able to survive at all. I see so much pain and terror and ugliness in my job. Sometimes, it's hard to remember that anything else exists.

Later I got the machete off the back of my pack and collected a bit of firewood. Solid fuel is fine for cooking when you are in a hurry or when every bit of wood is soaking wet, but it had been a hot, dry day and I like a campfire to sit beside at night. Mostly just gathered what I could pick up—tried to chop one piece in half with the machete, but when my head started spinning I decided that could wait for a day or so. It would be a small fire tonight. Not that I was planning to sit up very long anyway. Remade my sagging shelter and dug the groundsheet out of the pack. Threw a packet of dried chicken soup into the pot of rice boiling away on my fire. Made another cup of coffee when I finished eating, smeared repellent on all the exposed bits and sprawled beside the fire listening to the creek's quiet liquid noises. I watched the universe in the flames and glowing coals for a time before crawling into my lean-to for the night.

As I closed my eyes, I felt the bears at the edges of my mind, waiting for me. No—not again—not now. Then I pictured the deer as she'd stood and watched me and the bears dissolved. I'd never found anything before that could banish them once they chose to stalk me. Gratefully, I held the deer in my mind as I fell asleep.

Dawn comes quickly in the jungle. Light mist fading above the creek. A world of green of all shapes and shades, still wet with dew. A cicada gave its penetrating, drawn-out, single-note call over and over. I stuck only my head out from under the lean-to, not wanting to disturb this fragile, brief transition from night to day. A lone night heron flapped slowly past on his way to roost. I wondered where the deer was. A big beetle launched himself off a tree trunk and flew laboriously to land on the mosquito net beside me. The sun broke over the trees, gleaming off the 20-foot cohune palm fronds that hung over the creek. A kingfisher flew by, calling harshly, and as swiftly as it came, the dawn was gone and it was morning. I decided on fire again instead of solid fuel, I wasn't in any rush and wood smoke smells good in the morning air.

I spent that day and night and the following morning there, lying in the water or in the sun most of the time. The cool water took down some of the swelling around my stomach and back, and the sun baked a lot of the aches out. Gradually my shoulders felt just stiff instead of on fire. The third morning I even cautiously attempted a few gentle yoga poses. That loosened things up a bit. I'd brought my cleaning kit so I went over Beauty inch by inch and then cleaned my knife thoroughly as well.

The rain held off till the afternoon I left. Packed up, very gingerly put on my backpack, waded back down the creek to the Hummingbird Highway. The stolen Landrover was still on its nose at the bottom of the dropoff. No one seemed to have shown any interest in it yet. I debated, then simply walked along the highway for the three or four miles back to where I'd left the rental Land-rover at the Sibun River. It took awhile to start but the engine finally caught. I drove slowly and carefully back to the farm. I didn't want to deal with family yet, but I knew they'd be worrying by now. Also, I'd heal a lot faster with proper food and a good bed out of the weather.

"Auntie Tessa! Auntie Tessa do you got my blue duck?" "Auntie it's mine! I wannit!"

I was home. The Twins cannoned into my legs, thudding their heads into my stomach which brought tears of agony to my eyes and some most un-aunt-like language to my lips. I sagged against the Landrover as Ken crossed the yard in great strides and grabbed a twin in each arm.

"Tess! What's wrong? Are you hurt?" Then he yelled to Gayle and Sarah, "Here! Hang onto the kids while I get her into the house! He started to pick me up, sending waves of excruciating pain through me in the process.

I screamed. Ken let go like he'd grabbed a live coal as I yelled, "Let go! God! Let go! Please! It'll hurt more if you try to carry me, honest. Just let me hang onto your arm until I get my breath back. I'm really pretty well okay today—just not up to being leaped on yet!" I hung onto his arm and tried not to pass out.

"What happened, Sis? Is anything broken? Had I better get the doctor to come have a look at you? You don—"

"No doctor! Don't need one. Just bruised up and pulled a couple of tendons or something." I gave my prepared explanation, hoping it sounded convincing. "Was climbing up a steep hillside and a big rock came loose and I fell and it landed across my back. Had a hell of a job getting it off. Didn't feel like doing much after that so I just holed up for a couple of days. This morning it wasn't so bad so I decided to walk out and come home." I staggered into the house, holding onto Ken, and made it to my bed.

Ken flatly insisted on looking me over. I protested as much as I could, without seeming too strange about it, but finally had to let him. Sarah fussed and flapped and insisted they had to get me to a doctor immediately. I refused very firmly. Any doctor would recognize those grazes and that I couldn't afford. Ken looked thoughtful then said that, as it had been a couple of days since it had happened, I did not need a doctor. I silently blessed him for that pronouncement though it surprised me a little. He and Sarah cleaned and dressed the grazes and the worst of the cuts, gently rubbed liniment into my back, nearly killing me in the process, and poked assorted antibiotic and painkiller tablets as well as some hot soup down me before leaving me to sleep.

I was up and about the next day over their protests—I'd had three days to get used to it and a night in a real bed had done wonders. Grabbed all three local papers after breakfast. Jedson's assassination had been told to me over the breakfast table. I looked up from reading the first account to see Ken staring at me intently. He held my gaze for a moment then mumbled about work to be done and left the house. The papers were full of all sorts of speculations and wild theories. The Colombians were blamed, the CIA was blamed, the Honorable Opposition was blamed, Mexico was blamed, the Brits were blamed, and someone even managed to blame the Israelis—how, I never quite figured out. No one mentioned the two dead Cubans. Two unidentified dead men beside a green sedan at the Hummingbird Lumber Company yard were mentioned in small print on pages three, eight and nine respectively, but no one seemed to connect them in any way with Jedson. I noticed with a certain macabre humor that I had become "three unknown gunmen," "five or possibly six CIA agents" or "a troop of Colombian guerrilla fighters," depending on which newspaper one read. I smiled and had another cup of coffee.

I hadn't contacted Headquarters yet. Some bright boy in the police or at Airport Camp might be monitoring every radio wave they could for just such a contact. Headquarters would hear about

Jedson's death nearly as fast as if I contacted them anyway. I'd phone in when I could get into the city, as if I were calling to see about extending my vacation.

That evening, over dinner, Gayle and I discussed all the places we might visit during the rest of my stay. If I did everything she wanted to, I reckoned I'd need two years leave with full pay. We finally settled on hiring a boat and spending a week on the reef. She'd have to plead sick or something to get off school for that long but no one seemed worried.

That evening Ken maneuvered Sarah upstairs and me out onto the porch with the rum bottle and a couple of glasses. We chatted about everything and nothing. I got tired of waiting for whatever was on his mind.

"C'mon Ken. Spit it out. What's bugg'n you?" He hemmed and hawed awhile, then finally said, "Sis. You know I think a lot of you." Christ! Something serious for sure. That didn't sound like Ken and I started worrying. The farm? Gayle?

"I don't know how to say this. You know I'm not real clever with words. But Sis, I spent some time in New Orleans as you know. Work'n on the docks. That can get pretty rough sometimes. I've seen a lot of things more'n I should've maybe, and done more than I should've too. Never said anything before but I've thought for a long time you got yourself some mighty funny scars for a lady climber. Look an awful lot like some bullet holes and knife scars I've seen on some nasty customers on those docks. But you never came here hurt before. I don't like to see you hurt. Don't like to think of someone mak'n you hurt." He paused. I was wishing I was anywhere else, and cursing the Boss for ever sending me on this job. I didn't like the direction of this conversation one bit.

"You went off this time by yourself like you have before, only this time you come back hurt bad. And your eyes don't look—

right. This Jedson fella just got shot by someone. If you read the papers carefully, you see they got no idea who killed him. Way I figure it, that rock fell on you the same night he got bumped off. And that same night, you scraped yourself on some more rocks, three scrapes that if I didn't know better, I'd swear were bullet creases. I gotta feel'n you were mighty lucky those rocks didn't kill you."

The silence stretched between us. There was nothing to say. I rubbed one of the dogs behind the ears. Simply, literally, could not think of a word to say. Ken finally broke the silence. "You do things like this as a business, don't you? You're no reporter." I still said nothing. He shifted and sighed. "Guess I've known it for a long time—just didn't wanna know it, if you get my meaning. I 'spose you're CIA . . . hmm guess I don't really expect you to tell me outright. But—just one question I *do* want an answer to—why Jedson? Papers say he's a playboy, 't'aint no crime last I knew."

Well, at least now I knew why he'd agreed with me about no doctor. Christ, what a mess! What could I say? All those years of never leading a normal life for fear of compromising our security—all shot because I finally had to mix family and a job. At least he didn't disapprove, as long as I was on the "right" payroll. He'd been around enough to know the world didn't automatically provide safety and every society needed some people who worked outside the regular structures in order to protect its citizens. Decided to let him go on thinking I was CIA.

So, I said what I could, which wasn't much. "Jedson was a lot more than just a playboy. I can't tell you anything really, I'm sorry, but I'll have to ask you to believe me that Jedson *had* to be killed. I haven't disgraced the family name. I do earn my money though, and perhaps now you understand why I've not been too worried about saving up for my old age, why I've never married and had a pack of kids like Sarah always wants me to." I got up before he could ask me any more questions and went to bed, finally falling asleep near dawn.

The next day I drove into Belize City. Ken was out in the far pasture when I got up so I didn't speak with him again. It might have been better if I had, but I didn't.

The desk clerk at the Bellevue said they were sorry but they were full, the manager said they'd fit me in somehow and to leave my bag at the desk. I settled down with a cup of coffee and the telephone. Whatever god rules Belize's telephones was feeling magnanimous and I actually got through to the Boss in less than twenty minutes.

"Good morning, Tessa. How nice to hear your voice. Are you enjoying the sunshine?"

"Beautiful, Boss. In fact that's why I'm calling. If there's nothing too pressing, I'd like to extend my vacation for a week or ten days. My niece is twisting my arm to take her to the reef for a week. Had a minor climbing accident a few days ago and wouldn't mind lying in the sun for a week myself."

"I see no reason why you shouldn't. Things are quiet around the office right now so you can play hooky awhile longer. By the way, how's that flu you picked up just before you left? I trust all that sunshine has cleared it up?"

I had to laugh—nobody but the Boss would refer to someone breaking my cover and trying to kill me as "the flu"! "Fine now, cured completely." I knew he'd be almost as relieved as I was that there was no longer anyone who knew who and what I was or where I climbed—if he only knew that Ken had figured things out, he'd have a fit!

"Good. We'll see you in a week or two. If anything comes up before then, how can I contact you?"

"Can't. I'm going to be on a small boat in the middle of the Caribbean, a long ways from any phone!" I hung up fast, before he could order me to check in during the week—after all, I couldn't disobey orders if I never heard them.

Ordered another coffee and tried to phone my bank manager. The telephone god must've developed a headache. Three hours and several gallons of coffee later, I got through. Needn't have bothered. Paul's bills were being taken care of and were dropping.

Spent the afternoon finding a boat for Gayle and me. We could leave Saturday with a boatman I didn't know or on Monday with my favorite boatman, Robert. I decided on Monday. Ken was coming in on Saturday morning and was bringing Gayle with him. We could always find something to do over the weekend. Gayle liked Robert too and that could make all the difference to our trip.

The next week was a lovely dream. Robert is one of the best companions imaginable; born and raised on the island, he learned how to handle a boat before most kids can spell the word. We took camping gear and slept on a different beach every night. We lived on fresh coconuts and fish and lobster caught the same day, and the crispy fried bread that Robert made for every meal.

We swam and fished and explored the coral reefs by day, and sang and talked around a big fire by night. Robert had brought his guitar and a set of small drums for me to play. He'd nearly cried the first trip I took with him, when he found out I could play the drums and he didn't have his along. Gayle loves to sing, as does Robert (I can't carry a tune in a bucket despite being a pretty fair drummer). All in all we had some good sessions. Only once did it rain on us. A storm blew up very suddenly and we took refuge behind a small mangrove cay. Gayle and I took turns at bailing while Robert handled the boat. The storm blew itself out in a couple of hours. We spent a slightly soggy night, but the fried bread and coffee were just that much better the next morning. Gayle positively glowed the whole trip. I relaxed and healed and I was happy too. I could feel the tension draining out of me each day. I slept deeply and well for the first time in months, and no bears stalked my dreams, only a beautiful, delicate deer. I put on several pounds and my skin regained its normal sheen.

All good things end eventually and Sunday came too soon. Robert dropped us off at the Bellevue's private dock and carried our gear into the lobby. I paid him and thanked him once again. As we started up the stairs to my room, the man at the desk called me back to hand me an envelope. Just my name on it.

"A lady left this for you yesterday. She was most anxious that you get this the moment you returned. I hope it's not bad news?"

"I'm sure it's not serious. Thank you." I took it upstairs, unopened, with Gayle dying of curiosity beside me. But I didn't like it—there was no good reason for a letter to be waiting for me, so I insisted Gayle go take her shower and let me read it in peace. Fortunately. It was from Sarah.

Tessa, Ken has been kidnapped. I went over to my neighbor's for an hour with the Twins. When I got back he was gone. This paper was lying on the floor just inside the front door. I didn't know what to do but since it says not to notify anyone but you, I took the bus to town and left the Twins with my sister, as I was afraid for them to stay at the farm, and I am leaving this for you at the hotel. I will go back now to the farm so as to be there if they want to contact me again. I am afraid to ask anyone to stay with me because they said I must tell no one but you. I am very frightened. Sarah.

The other piece of paper, folded and smudged and tearstained, said simply:

Tell sister-in-law her brother is kidnapped. Tell no one other or you want be killed.

My mind went numb. I read Sarah's note again. "I am very frightened." That must be the understatement of the year. She brought the Twins to town by bus, because she was afraid to learn to drive though Ken had offered to teach her many times. Gone back to stay alone at the farm. The farm isn't completely isolated as the Cayo Valley is pretty built up by Belizean standards, but the nearest neighbor was half a mile down the road and you couldn't see any other houses from theirs. I didn't think Sarah had ever spent a night there alone before. She always went with Ken if he had to be gone overnight or else stayed with her sister. Now she was waiting, alone, waiting for whoever was either strong enough or well enough armed to capture Ken to come back. I wondered if he was still alive, and if he'd known why he'd been taken.

Then Gayle came bouncing out of the bathroom, half dried with a towel wrapped around her, demanding to know what was in the letter. She left damp wet prints on the floor. She stopped bouncing when she saw my face. I tried to pull myself together as I took her hand and pulled her over to sit on the bed beside me. "What . . . is something wrong? You look all funny."

I put my arms around her while I tried to find the right words but they wouldn't come. How do you tell a child that her father has been kidnapped and is in danger? While she was still in the shower I'd decided I had to tell her that much at least. I finally wound up giving her the letter and note to read.

Strange, the things your memory chooses to hold—my clothes growing damp as I held her to me, damp from tears as well as shower water—a trapped fly buzzing monotonously against the window as a young girl learned fear. I waited. The fly tired and crawled along the casement. Water dripped from the ends of her hair onto my arm. When her sobs began to slow I pulled her to her feet and half carried her to the washbasin and wiped her face with a wet washcloth, trying not to remember how I first learned fear. That I should now, even indirectly, be the cause of Gayle's meeting real fear for the first time—I'm convinced that the Three Sisters of Fate are sadistic bitches.

When she could talk, she asked, "But . . . but why? Why would anybody kidnap my Dad? I don't understand." She looked so confused and pathetically young. And suddenly it was like a time warp, and I couldn't answer for a moment because the hot African sun was burning down on me and an African woman was wiping my tears away while the bodies of my mother and Uncle Jawa decomposed in the room behind me. Then Gayle's face was there again, waiting for an answer she could comprehend. So I said, "I don't know either, but kidnappers usually want money so I guess. . . ."

"But he doesn't have lots of money!"

"Maybe they don't know that."

"He . . . he isn't dead or hurt or—or anything is he?"

"Of course not!" I tried desperately to sound convincing. "After all, they wouldn't be able to trade him for money if he was dead, would they?" Ken might very well be dead. Well, we'd deal with that when and if we came to it.

"You have a lot of money, don't you?" The sudden hope lit up her face and I damn near cried myself but that would really have panicked her.

"Some. We'll just have to see whether I have enough or not. Maybe I can borrow enough. Won't know until they get in touch with us again."

"We could sell the cows 'n stuff couldn't we? And . . . and my horse." She took off the pearl necklace I'd given her and handed it to me, telling me to sell it too. I've never felt prouder of anyone. Then the tears came again and she hurled herself against me sobbing wildly. I held her till the storm was spent. We talked for a while after that, and I was going to give her back her necklace, but thought it might be a little easier for her if she thought she was helping in some way and I kept it, promising her I'd get her another one for Christmas if we did have to sell it.

The first thing was to get her safely out of the way. The Twins were safe with Sarah's sister and Gayle would be too, but I didn't trust her not to turn up at the farm at the wrong moment. The Twins didn't know anything was wrong but Gayle did and she was cussedly independent. I decided I'd feel a lot happier with her a long way away. Blade would take her in. Told her she was going abroad to stay with a friend of mine. She was missing a lot of school but that couldn't be helped. Called the desk and asked them to get me the overseas operator.

I got first Headquarters, then the Intelligence Department, and finally Blade. It was such a relief to hear his deep voice answer the phone after his secretary got him for me.

"Tessa! This is a pleasant surprise! What can I do for you?" Even on a telephone some semblence of security had to be kept.

"Blade, I've got a tremendous favor to ask you."

"Ask and you shall receive! At least if it's humanly possible!"

"I'm in Belize, visiting my brother and his family. Some family problems have come up, serious ones, and I want my niece, Gayle, to come and stay with you until we get things sorted out at this end. Don't know how long it'll be for, but I'd like to put her on the 2:00 plane this afternoon if I can get a seat for her. 'Fraid she'll be arriving with just the clothes she's wearing. I'd like to ask you to buy her some things and let me pay you later. I know I'm asking a lot but it'd really be a tremendous relief to me to know she's with you. Can you do it?" Please, please keep Gayle safe for me! I wanted to beg, but not over a public telephone.

"Yes, of course! If she's half as marvelous a kid as you've always said she is, it will be a pleasure. But what's wrong?"

"You're wonderful, as always! Thanks a million. She'll explain when she gets there. I'll call you back in half an hour and let you know her arrival time. Bye." I hung up before he could ask anything more.

The Assassin and the Deer

I told Gayle my friend's name was Blade and she asked what kind of a name that was. I explained it was a sort of nickname—his real name was an Afghani name, which roughly translated as "Shining Blade of Allah." Unfortunately my attempts to pronounce it had translated as approximately "Unclean Pig in the Garden of Allah." Fortunately Blade saw the funny side of it and, as none of his other new friends could pronounce his name correctly either, he gave up and suggested we just leave it in English and shorten it to Blade. Gayle giggled and said she still thought it was a funny sort of name, and I was glad of anything that took her mind off her father, even for a moment. I knew Blade would see to it that she was never left alone, would take off work if he could, get a secretary to take care of her if he did have to spend any time at the office. He knew all about children losing parents (Christ I hoped it wouldn't come to that!) and about being afraid for your family, and he'd make it as easy for her as anyone could. I thanked whatever gods may be that I'd been able to reach him.

Several hours later I'd made all arrangements to get Gayle on the right connecting flight and seen her onto the plane, asking one of the stewardesses to look after her. Blade was going to be very upset once Gayle told him what was going on. He'd be able to guess what was really involved. I just hoped he wouldn't contact the Boss. With luck he'd assume I had done so and that a team was even now on its way to Belize.

Once I got back to my hotel room, I locked the door and got out my radio. Codes are a pain but for once I was glad of such things. If someone was listening, they'd know I'd called someone but at least they wouldn't know who or why. Took me ages to get my messages coded properly. Good thing Dave couldn't see me—he's head of Communications Department and can't believe that anyone who can calculate bullet trajectories can't use codes fluently. He keeps yell'n at me *to learn*. I've tried and tried but I'm still ridiculously slow. At least it means I'm automatically assigned the best radio man available when I need one. In fact if it's a heavy job involving very many lives, Dave usually comes along as well, says I can't *afford* to have my radio man killed and it's well known that nothing but a polar bear or a harpoon can kill an Eskimo, so nobody's gonna kill him very easily. (Personally I attribute Dave's tendency to remain untouched by bullets to his Green Beret training and fast reflexes rather than his pure-blood Eskimo ancestry.)

I threw the code book down and opened up the back of my "radio alarm clock" and flipped the switch to warm up the miniaturized radio set. Finally, got Bobby on the air.

"You good for anything besides training? Over."

The answer came as a two-letter group followed by a four-letter group followed by an eight-letter group—knowing Bobby, I didn't bother to decode it before replying.

"I need help." Fortunately, Bobby knows I hate coding and decoding so he didn't ask questions, just replied, "Roger" in clear.

"Get to Belize tomorrow noon latest. Fancy dress. Bellevue Hotel. Operational from time of landing. Do not, repeat—do not, inform anyone else."

"Roger and out."

I was so lucky to have Bobby to call on—no questions. He'd come because I asked him to. Supposed I should have gone to the Boss, but in a way this was private, and besides, I didn't want a whole team down here, which is what he'd insist on since it was a kidnapping. Belize is too small for a team to go unnoticed and that could lead to some very big problems. Could also get my brother killed—if he wasn't dead already.

Nothing to do now but wait. Wished I could go to the farm but I didn't dare. The ball wouldn't start rolling till I did, and I didn't want it to before I had Bobby behind me. Sarah would have to spend a second night alone, waiting. Went to bed early but couldn't sleep. Recriminations and gruesome mental images plagued me. And I panicked about Sarah—would the kidnapper take her, too, now that she'd delivered the note? I sincerely wished I'd chosen any other line of work. And I kept wondering, who? Had Guiterra lied to me? I was sure he'd broken completely. Had there been a third guard with Jedson? Had Guiterra informed someone about me after all? I didn't know enough to make any sort of a sound guess but that didn't stop me from trying throughout the night.

Morning came and went eventually. Sat in the lobby reading the papers after I'd dragged out lunch as long as I could. When Bobby arrived I hardly recognized him—he was perfect. An aging Hippie-type backpacker who wandered through the door, checked the prices and left without even a glance in my direction. I got up and went out a few minutes later. When no one was nearby, I walked past him slowly, speaking without looking at him.

"Get a cab to the cemetery. Start walking out the main road out of town from there. I'll pick you up in about an hour."

There was no reply and I expected none. I walked on to the market, bought some fruit and returned to the hotel. When I checked out I said I'd probably be back in a couple of days but I didn't know exactly when.

There was no one in sight when I stopped for Bobby a couple of miles past the cemetery. It's a long drive to the farm from Belize City, so I had plenty of time to fill Bobby in on what he needed to know. He was delighted—overjoyed—to be operational again and was raring to go. Wished I felt that way. I'd seen a lot of people sweating over missing relatives but somehow never imagined it could be me. Bobby put it very succinctly.

"Look, I know 'e's your brother but you're gonna hafta forget 'e is. I don't give a hoot in hell about 'im myself but I don't want to hafta start worry'n 'bout you. You get yourself killed if you

worry too much 'n I never did fancy funerals as entertainment.''
He was right of course.

I stopped about a mile down the road from the farm and gave
Bobby directions. Then I drove on past and into Cayo. Killed time
buying groceries, since Sarah was probably getting low by now,
and getting gas. Stopped and had a coffee, buying and rereading
the same papers I'd read that morning. But they made an excuse
to hang around over my coffee. Got back to the farm turnoff two
hours after dropping Bobby. There were two sticks laid in a vee
shape on the road that hadn't been there earlier, which was Bobby's way of telling me no one was hiding in the bushes waiting to
shoot me.

I drove the Landrover right up to the front door anyway. Interrupted Sarah's wails and ''Thank God's'' by handing her two big
sacks of groceries to hold while I darted out to get my stuff.
Bobby's stick or no, I felt much better once I shut the door behind
us, locking it, I hoped, unobtrusively.

I tried to comfort Sarah but after a while, when her spate of
hysterics didn't show any sign of letting up, I went and made tea
and a couple of good solid sandwiches. Practically had to hold her
nose and force them down, but once she started eating she was
amazed at how hungry she was. When I asked, she thought a
moment then replied she guessed she hadn't eaten since she found
Ken missing. We talked for a while after she finished. I told her
where Gayle was and promised any help I could give, then insisted
she take a stiff drink and go to bed. She hadn't slept at all and was
about done in. When I checked on her half an hour later she was
snoring softly.

Nothing more for me to do but wait until five. I was glad she'd
had the sense to leave the Twins with her sister—don't know how
I'd have coped with them too.

Eventually the hands of the clock dragged around. Sarah was

still sleeping. Left a note saying I'd gone for a walk and would be back soon. Didn't want her waking up to find me missing too. The dogs whined when I left them behind.

There is a hill in the back pasture which sits by itself. The land all around is cleared, as is most of the hill, but there are a few large rocks and some bushes at the top. Bobby was waiting there as I'd told him to. He'd expected to be camping out so had brought what he needed with him, hence the Hippie backpacker disguise. Bobby with long hair and a matted beard just didn't look like Bobby. I shook my head. He looked at me a little self-consciously.

"Well, you did say fancy dress. Thought it was quite good meself."

"Oh it's excellent, just takes some getting used to."

"Worse for me, this damn beard is hot 'n it itches! Anyhow, haven't seen anyone yet but found a spot where someone's been sett'n regular. Just beyond those trees." He pointed to a grove of fruit trees that ended near the yard. "Good view of the house from there."

I looked over the terrain while Bobby continued.

"Think I'll move over t'other side of the house. Maybe set behind that small shed at the far end. Checked earlier and I can see anyone even think'n 'bout going into those trees. Then I'll be close 'nough to warn you when 'e's com'n."

He didn't add "close enough to help if you need it" but I knew he was thinking it. Sounded good to me. I decided to move the Landrover away from the house a bit when I got back, so it would be more obvious from the trees. I wanted Ken's kidnapper to know I'd arrived.

Brought out the hip flask of rum I'd brought from the house but Bobby laughed and said that was the first stop he'd had the taxi driver make. He produced two bottles of Bacardi from the depths of his pack with a satisfied grin. I sighed and hoped Bobby wouldn't pick now to go on a bender. He didn't very often. Always drank a lot but it never seemed to affect him, except every once in a while, when he did a thorough job of it. And he hadn't been operational for many years. Wondered for a second if I should've called the Boss instead. Too late now. Bobby opened a bottle and passed it to me. We drank slowly, in silence, until it was nearly dark and I had to leave.

Sarah was still asleep when I got back. Moved the Landrover out into plain sight. Brought the dogs inside and fed them. Bobby would be in place beside the shed now. The dogs caught my tension and wouldn't settle down.

I waited in Ken's darkened study with Beauty propped beside me, though I left the lights on in the kitchen and living room. The kidnapper had to know we were at home but I wasn't about to sit by an open window in a lit-up room.

It was nearly ten o'clock when I heard an owl hoot from over by the shed and knew that whoever we were waiting for was on his way in. I waited immobile—listening—straining to hear him.

Nothing. Night noises and the house settling. I was glad Sarah was asleep. Time stretched and crawled. Nothing. Glad Bobby was out there. Just prayed he wasn't drunk. Ten-thirty. Was that . . . ? No, dog shifting in the next room. Crickets. Nothing.

A hideous bawling of terror and mortal agony shattered the night. Sarah screamed. I grabbed Beauty and raced upstairs to her room. She was sitting bolt upright, hands clenched at her sides, screaming with a terror equal to that of whatever was dying outside. I grabbed her shoulders and shook her but she kept on screaming, so I finally slapped her across the face. Seemed cruel, but I had to break through that total terror somehow. The screams changed to whimpers and she sagged forward, so I put my arms around her and held her as I'd held Gayle not 24 hours before, while the noise outside slowly died. The silence afterwards was almost worse than the noise. Sarah whimpered softly, asking what had happened.

"I'm not certain but I think our friend left us a little present just to upset us and tell us he means business."

"A . . . present? I . . . I don't understand." Then Sarah suddenly saw Beauty lying on the bed where I'd dropped her. I slapped a hand over Sarah's mouth before she could get the scream out.

"No. No, it's alright. It's okay. You'll be alright. Now listen to me, please." I took my hand away and she nodded slightly, still staring at Beauty as if the gun was a cobra on her bed. I hastily laid it out of sight on the floor. "Look, someone just killed a large animal out there, probably one of the cows. That same person has Ken. I'll go see what happened in a minute. The gun's okay, I . . . borrowed it a . . . from a friend in town. I know Ken has one but I want you to keep that in the house." That sounded pretty thin, seeing how she felt about guns, but it was the best I could do on the spur of the moment and she seemed to accept it, so I went on hastily, "Now, sit tight for a bit. Don't scream again no matter WHAT you see or hear. Unless someone besides me tries to come into this room—then scream bloody murder!"

I called the two Dobermans into her room, as they might slow the man down if he tried anything, and they'd make her feel safer, too. I left the Alsatian on patrol downstairs. Fortunately, their bedroom door had a heavy bolt on the inside, so I told her to bolt it after me and stay well back from the window but to keep an ear open for anyone trying to climb up to it. It was shut, but too flimsy to do any good. Told her again not to scream unless someone tried to come into her bedroom—to keep quiet even if someone got into the rest of the house. She was too terrified to object much, though she didn't like the thought of my going outside. I didn't particularly either, but whoever was out there would expect me to, so, since I didn't want him to think I might have someone around to tell me when it was safe, I went out.

I took Beauty and went back downstairs, into Gayle's empty room, eased out her window and sprinted for the Landrover. No one shot at me. Drove out across the pasture in the direction the sound had come from. Through a gate—I'd repair that in daylight, no way was I getting out of that Landrover just to open a stick gate. That Landrover was the only option I had of changing my mind in a hurry. Halfway across the next pasture something showed in the headlights.

The calf wasn't quite dead yet. Its hind legs were tied to a rough tripod of sticks. Its head and shoulders were on the ground under the pile of its intestines. A couple of carrion beetles were already at work, not even waiting for it to finish dying. A disembowelled animal, or person, lives for a horribly long time. I shot it quickly and drove back to the house at top speed, trying to tell myself that if the man had wanted to harm Sarah he could have long before this. But he could have killed the calf before too. He'd waited till I came. Told myself Bobby would make sure Sarah was alright. Then I heard the dogs barking ferociously.

A panic-stricken cow raced in front of me. I slammed the brakes and wrenched the wheel. Then I was in the yard and out of the Landrover at a dead run, missing the note on the living room floor entirely as I raced upstairs. Banged on the bedroom door calling Sarah. Heard her answer and about collapsed with relief. The door flew open and she was hugging me and crying. Once she calmed down enough to listen, I told her one of this year's calves was dead and not to go out in the morning until I had a chance to get it buried.

We went downstairs. The note was lying just inside the front door. Must've nearly stepped on it on the way in. It was on the same sort of paper as the first and in pencil again. I picked it up, holding it so Sarah could read it too.

You brother die same way unless bring $50,000.00 in small bills tomorrow night.

An owl hooted and I relaxed. We were safe for now. Wished I could tell Sarah we were safe, but I didn't feel I could risk it—what she didn't know she couldn't give away accidentally—or be forced to tell.

Talk and food and bed. I slept solidly, knowing Bobby was on guard outside. Met him behind the shed just before dawn with a thermos of hot coffee. He was living on tinned stuff straight from the can as he didn't want to risk a fire. Showed him the note and we discussed what to do. He would move into the shed temporarily while I buried the calf and got Sarah and I some breakfast. I would take her to town with me partly because I'd need her at the bank, and partly so Bobby could use the house for the day, get a wash and a good, comfortable sleep. We were sure there'd be no further developments before Sarah and I returned that evening.

The ground was stony and burying that calf was no easy job. Until then, I'd mainly felt fear, first for Ken and later for Sarah. As I swung the pick-ax beside the mutilated calf, the anger came boiling up, overwhelming the fear. I shovelled out the loosened stuff and swung the pick-ax again. The bluebottle flies made a revolting cloud around the calf. So bloated they could hardly fly, they kept veering into me and trying to settle on my hair and face. Blisters grew and so did my anger. This wasn't the first time I'd seen gutted or decapitated animals staked out to terrify the owners. But this time it was an innocent animal gutted to terrify *my* family. Doubly glad now Gayle was far away with Blade. Glad I'd brought the dogs in last night too. How would the next message come tonight? Another calf? Better put the horses in the kitchen tonight.

Make a hell of a mess but I'd rather that than bury one of them tomorrow. Then a vision of Ken strung up like the calf crawled into my mind and left me sick and shaking. Shut Ken out of my mind, no good wondering. But my hands were still shaking when I cut the calf down and heaved it into the shallow hole. Pushed its guts in as well and shovelled dirt over the lot, hating the man who'd made the job necessary more than I'd hated anyone for a long time.

The trip to town was made in virtual silence. Once Sarah asked how the calf had been killed. I figured not knowing was better than being able to envision her husband the same way, so I just said it was bad. She knew that much anyway from my silence. I kept seeing that calf and just couldn't think of anything to say to cheer Sarah up.

Naturally, there was no way we could possibly raise $50,000 in one day. What money I had would take several days to clear if I wrote Sarah a check. So we took out every cent Sarah and Ken had. Fortunately they had a joint account. That amounted to a little over $6,000. Nowhere near what the man asked for, but it would still make an impressive looking pile in small bills. I doubted the man would realize immediately that it wasn't all he'd asked for. After all, how many people know what $50,000 in small bills looks like? Hopefully a few minutes would be all Bobby and I would need. It was the best we could do anyway. Getting the money from the bank took time and much convincing of the assistant manager that Sarah wasn't taking Ken's money and leaving. Finally succeeded without telling him what the score was. By the time we finished changing the bills into smaller notes, a few at a time at different stores, it was time for lunch. I deliberately took Sarah to a seafood restaurant that was renowned for excellent food—and very slow service.

Managed to kill nearly two hours over lunch. Then I stalled by doing a little shopping and checking at the hotel for messages. Someone had called several times from abroad, that would be Blade. Considered returning his call but decided against it—nothing I could tell him that wouldn't worry him even more than he was already.

By the time we left town it was nearly four o'clock. I didn't exactly burn up the road going home either, so the clock was pushing six before we drove in. I didn't want to arrive after dark but wanted to give Bobby just as long as possible since he'd be up all night again. The sticks were in the driveway again so I drove straight in.

Left Sarah to unload the groceries while I went to get the horses. She was horrified at the thought of two big horses in her kitchen but agreed when I reminded her of the calf's fate. Ken's horse allowed himself to be led into the kitchen and tethered to the sink but Gayle's Arabian was a different matter—it'd gone full dark before I finally succeeded in dragging that beast in and I had an extremely sore shinbone, thanks to it giving me a nasty kick when halfway through the kitchen door.

I needed a bath, kidnapper or no. Had time for a bath and dinner and innumerable hands of Canasta with Sarah before the man made his appearance. We played cards in Ken's study as I wanted us well out of the way of any windows. Would have felt trapped in a solid room with only one entrance if I hadn't known Bobby was outside. As it was, Bobby's hoot came only a couple of minutes before the crash. Sarah jumped up, sending the cards flying, as I hurriedly motioned her to keep silent and strained to hear. The crash had sounded like one of the front windows. Couldn't hear anything for the din made by the dogs and horses. Gradually the night quieted. I waited a few more minutes. Bobby didn't hoot again but neither could I hear the man anywhere. Took Beauty with me though I didn't plan to use her—would do me no good to shoot the only link I had with Ken. I eased my way out of the study, down the hall until I could see through into the living room. Blood on the floor—a lot of blood. Heard a sound in the hall behind me and whirled around, dropping and starting a vicious kick before I realized it was Sarah. She froze and stared at me like she'd never seen me before. Well, in a way she hadn't. I stood up, feeling a bit shaky, and motioned her back into the study but she came up beside me. She took one look, saw the blood and fainted dead away, so I carried her back to the study. Laid her on the rug and shut the door firmly as I left. I'd hear anyone trying to open it.

Was surveying what I could of the living room from the hall without exposing myself when I heard a funny sort of half hoot. What? Then it came again. I was certain it was Bobby, but it wasn't his normal signal and he'd called twice . . . maybe? . . . was he hurt? . . . then I thought I knew what he was trying to tell me. The man must've drawn back a ways from the house but not left entirely. Hoped that was what Bobby meant anyway. I stepped out into the living room, expecting to be shot at any second. Wondering if I'd know when it came. Wondering if Bobby could stop the man—I could imagine him raising the rifle and sighting on my head, and wondered where Bobby was if that was what was happening.

I was still alive, so I looked around. Blood everywhere. Broken glass everywhere. A sheet of paper was stuck over a glass shard sticking up from the bottom of the window. I waded through the mess and retrieved tonight's communication feeling appallingly vulnerable outlined against the window by the living room light. But I was still alive as I stepped past the edge of the window and collapsed against the wall to read what I held in my hand.

I heard a sound from the study and raced in. Might be a bit upsetting to come to all alone in the study when the last thing you'd seen was your living room full of blood. Whoever Ken's kidnapper was, he certainly had dramatic ideas of how to deliver a simple note—ones that took a lot of cleaning up too.

Sarah was just sitting up as I entered. The first thing she wanted to know was whose blood it was and if I thought it might be Ken's. I pointed out that the blood was very fresh so it couldn't have been carried far. Hadn't coagulated yet. And there was no place nearby where it would be feasible to keep a prisoner, so Ken was out as the donor. Didn't tell her that Bobby had searched the entire area around the farm thoroughly and if Ken were being held nearby he would have found him. Told her I imagined a neighbor lost a couple of chickens tonight. In fact, later, as I was cleaning up the mess I found a blood-soaked feather. Then she saw the paper I was holding, so we read it together.

You have money—turn main room light off—on.

I went out and did so. Waited. No hoot so he was still around. Wished I'd thought to lock the dogs in another room. They'd been busy with the fresh blood.

Scolded them and made them lie down in one corner of the room so they couldn't track it around. For a long time the only sounds were the dogs licking each other and the horses shifting in the kitchen. Then I became aware of a soft steady sound from the study and realized Sarah was praying. They say there are no atheists in foxholes, but one thing I couldn't have done at the moment was pray. Not with the kidnapper still outside.

The faintest sound and then it came. A dark shape flew through the broken window. I dived back into the hall and braced for the explosion but none came. After a moment I cautiously raised my head and crept back to the doorway. A decapitated cat lay on the floor with a paper tied around its middle with a piece of string. The dogs were going berserk. At first I thought it was the cat, Sesame, that lived in the shed, and felt thoroughly sick. I'd not even tried to bring her into the house because she was a very wild, independent creature that no one had ever been able to lay hands on. Someone had now. Wondered how he'd managed to. The head had been neatly severed—not by a machete, looked more like a garrotte had been used. I felt numb. No one had ever gotten that close to Sesame before. As I turned the body over to untie the string I saw a patch of white fur. Sesame was gray all over. I felt almost lightheaded with relief. The man was insane, I was convinced, but he couldn't catch Sesame. He'd had to catch someone else's gray cat.

Somehow that small fallibility relieved me immensely. But not Sarah. It was the final straw for her. She started to sob. No screams. Just quiet sobs that went on and on without end or change. I couldn't bring myself to slap her out of it this time. I didn't think it would work anyway. Too much horror, for too long, for a person who was totally unprepared for anything of the kind. I read the latest message alone.

You bring money in Landrover Guacamayo Bridge tomorrow. You at Bridge exactly 12 noon. You be alone and unarmed. You come early or late or anyone with you or follow you, you brother die.

And I would die if I did as told. Unless Bobby was as good as he used to be. If he wasn't, I was going to be very dead tomorrow. Not a pleasant thought but there was nothing I could do about Bobby, so I started the long business of cleaning up after I led Sarah back to the study. Put the cat's body in a plastic bag. Wiped the dogs down as best I could and tied them in the hallway. I'd bathe them in the morning. Was starting on the living room when Bobby hooted all clear. Every time I carried a bucket into the kitchen to empty it, or bloody cloths to wash out, the horses shied and snorted at the smell. An hour later the living room looked fairly presentable except for the empty window frame. Sarah had been so proud of having a real picture window, such things being few and far between in Belize. She hadn't even noticed it was broken. She was still crying when I checked on her after cleaning up. Told her I was going out for a quick look around but I don't think she even heard me.

Took the note out to Bobby, who greeted me with relief, obscenities, and a wave of rum fumes.

"What the fuck's been go'n on? Looked like 'e 'as carry'n a bucket when 'e went past me then I heard one hell of a crash, then 'e comes by again but hangs around, then the light goes off 'n comes on again 'n 'e goes in again carrying someth'n this time too. Then 'e goes away 'n I hoot 'n you don' show till now!! Nearly came in looking for ya but heard you quiet'n the dogs so I guessed you was still alive at least. Hadn't a clue from straight up what was go'n on." He glared at me. Hadn't occurred to me that Bobby might've been worried. Made me feel better.

"Sorry, didn't mean to worry you. Anyway, probably was a bucket. He redecorated Sarah's living room in chicken blood. Left a note saying to flip the lights if we had the money, so I did. Then he slung a cat that lost its head somewhere through the window with a note tied to its middle. I've got it with me, the note that is. Then it took awhile to clean everything up. Kept hoping Sarah would go to bed but she's flipped out and can't do anything but cry. Cat was the final straw."

Bobby looked thoughtful. Poured himself a cup from the thermos I'd brought and read the last message by flashlight.

"I don' like it. This character is fucked-up-crazy. All this stuff with dead animals 'n blood 'n stuff. 'N 'e's out to get you. Gotta feel'n 'e wants you real bad. 'N if 'e ever do catch up with you I don't think 'e wants to offer you a cuppa tea either. You sure you don' know this guy personal like?"

"I've told you all I know! Might've tangled with him sometime or he may just be pissed off at my killing some of his buddies, least I'm assuming he's something to do with this last job. Must be. Wish I knew if it were just one guy or if he's got friends with him.''

"Well, if 'e does I sure hope they ain't crazy too! One's 'nough."

I agreed wholeheartedly!

I didn't want to leave Sarah alone for very long so went right back. She was still crying exactly where I'd left her, so I hauled her to her feet and half carried her upstairs, undressed her and put her to bed. A couple of hours later when I checked on her, she was still crying. Didn't look like she'd moved a muscle. I didn't do too well in the sleep department either.

Got up when it was light enough to see to take the horses out. No sign of Sarah yet, so I cooked Bobby a hot breakfast. Took it out to him, told him to get some sleep and meet me in the driveway out of sight of the house at 9:30 A.M., assuming our friend wasn't around.

Cleaned the horse shit out of the kitchen. Got myself some breakfast. One dog bathed and two to go when Sarah appeared, red-eyed and pale but no longer crying. I got her a cup of coffee and then bathed the remaining dogs. I was exhausted and sick of the smell of blood and dead animals. Sick with worry, too—and fear. Fear of dying in a couple of hours time. Fear of what the crazy might do to Ken—or had already done. I tried to pull myself together for Sarah's sake, and then felt better myself.

We got Sarah some breakfast and talked. I had another coffee to keep her company. She seemed pretty much herself this morning—worn out and very worried, but functioning and thinking again. I showed her the last message, saying I'd leave at 9:30 A.M. With luck Ken would be home for dinner. God, I hoped he would be. Wished I felt half as confident of that as I made out to Sarah. I was awfully afraid he was long dead. There was no need to have kept him alive to get the money and me—as long as I didn't know for certain, I'd have to do as I was told. But he might still be alive. The kidnapper was crazy. With luck he'd want me to see Ken die before he killed me. For that he would have to keep Ken alive in the meantime. I felt like Bobby did though—a crazy scared me a lot worse than any professional. I'd seen some things that insanity could do when it was blood-crazy and I was beginning to feel like I was trapped in one of my worse nightmares.

I decided to leave Sarah at the neighbors with strict instructions to take the Twins and leave the country immediately if I didn't come back that night. Gave her the Boss's number to call the minute she got off the plane. The Organization would give her a new identity if I didn't show up after a while and there would be plenty of money. She already had Blade's number so she could contact Gayle. Might all be for nothing if it took Bobby and me a day or so to sort out, but if the man got us there was nothing to stop him from doing whatever his twisted mind could dream up to Sarah, and the Twins too, if he could find them. Had a feeling he'd make a clean sweep of my family if he could. Blessed Blade again for taking Gayle in. At least he couldn't get her. Then I suddenly wondered how my big, rough, tough Afghani rebel was doing as a babysitter. The thought of Blade and Gayle getting to know each other made me want to smile for the first time since I found out Ken was kidnapped.

Sarah was very upset at my instructions but finally promised to do as told. Unfortunately, I couldn't convince her without her realizing just how unsure I was of the outcome. She kept repeating, "But surely he'll let Ken go when you give him the money!" I couldn't explain so I reminded her of how peculiarly he'd acted so far and she finally gave in. She didn't like my going alone but the note made it clear there was no choice. Wished I could've told her

Bobby would be with me—close behind anyway.

When we finished doing the breakfast dishes, I asked Sarah for any old newspapers she had, explaining that I wanted to cut them into dollar-bill-sized pieces to pad out the $6,000 we had. She helped me and soon we had a much more respectable looking bag of "money."

The top two layers were solid money but the packets below just had a bill top and bottom, the rest was newspaper. Looked okay to a casual inspection and it hefted right. Best we could do.

Changed out of my bloody clothes and into old fatigues and put on my jungle boots before I left. Borrowed Ken's sheath knife. A long-sleeved shirt in the middle of a hot day would look very suspicious so I couldn't use my arm sheath. I stuck my knife down one boot and Ken's down the other, hoping that in the event of a search he'd quit after finding one. Wishful thinking probably.

Wound my garrote around my bun and tucked it under out of sight. A beehive hairdo might be searched but for some reason a tightly wound bun never is. Stuck Beauty in the bottom of the money bag when Sarah wasn't looking—didn't want her to know I was taking a gun when the note said Ken would be killed if I showed up with one. Not that I was intending to meet the guy armed, Bobby would carry Beauty as well as his gun, and if the need and the opportunity came, he could pass her to me later on. Nine o'clock. Loaded Sarah and her overnight case into the Landrover as well as the money and left. Bobby would wonder when I didn't stop but he'd see Sarah in the car and guess what was going on. No sign of him. Left Sarah off at her neighbor's explaining that Ken and I would be away overnight camping and would they please put her up. If we got back that night, well and good; if not, no explanations would be necessary. Just hoped Sarah wouldn't act too out of character. She'd promised to behave naturally, but she'd deserve an Emmy Award if she really managed to.

I picked Bobby up a few minutes later. Told him the arrangements I'd made for Sarah. He approved the newspaper "money" and transferred Beauty to his sack. It's a long, bumpy, muddy trip to the Guacamayo Bridge. Right up into the mountains past the San Luis logging camp, then down an old logging road that winds its way deeper and deeper into the interior. Mostly tall grass and stunted pine trees. Where there's a pocket of limestone, the jungle takes over but it can't survive on the granite-based soil that covers most of the higher bits of the Maya Mountains. Normally I enjoy the mountains. Today I didn't have much interest in the scenery, not even when a flock of parakeets flew alongside the Landrover for a moment before veering off in a flurry of green feathers and much squawking.

Bobby chattered until I asked him to shut up, then accused me of being an unfriendly bitch. A moment later he grinned, patting my shoulder, and said, "Okay, okay, I'll be quiet before you do me an injury or run off the road or someth'n. Anyone would think you were nervous, the way you're acting."

And I thought, "anyone listening to you chatter just now would think *you* were, Bobby," but I kept silent. Wondered if the thought of me being nervous worried him half as much as the thought of his being nervous worried me.

At least he wasn't likely to get killed out of the deal. The trip continued in silence. Crawled the last four or five miles as silently as possible, coasting wherever I could. Sound carries a long ways in that sort of country and I didn't want the man to realize I stopped for a while a mile before the bridge. Bobby bailed out and I gave him co-ordinates for the bridge and described the surrounding topography briefly. Fortunately I'd hiked in the area before and knew it pretty well. We wished each other luck and I watched him disappear behind the nearest hill.

Allowed half an hour for him to get close to the bridge and find a spot to wait unseen. Not much time but he didn't need to find the guy, just stay out of sight himself. With the tall grass and numerous water courses he should manage.

I drove onto the bridge at 12:00 exactly.

Got out slowly with my hands in view, walked ten feet ahead of the Landrover and stood with my hands up. Waited. My back kept expecting a bullet. Seconds stretched like hours. A deer fly buzzed around me briefly. Silence, except for the breeze and the water gurgling around the rocks and under the bridge. A vulture circled high above. The butterflies my arrival had scared away came back to drink from the puddle at the end of the bridge. Bobby should be somewhere on the hillside behind me. If Ken was with the man, Bobby would shoot. If not, he was to play it by ear, as long as he didn't kill the man before Ken was found. Wondered what Headquarter's computer would say my life expectancy was just then. My arms began to ache. I wondered if the man was watching me and whether he would show himself or just deliver another message. I hoped not, as picking up Bobby again, unseen, might present problems. A couple of butterflies flew away and others took their place. I lowered my arms, sitting down slowly at the same time. If he was here, he'd seen I was unarmed. No point in waiting around all day holding my hands in the air. I watched the water flowing under the bridge and wished my guts would stop churning.

Five minutes later I saw a movement behind a rock at the water's edge. A small, slim man carrying a Soviet AKM walked over to the bridge. He motioned me to stand up. I did so, with my hands in the air again. No sign of Ken, but neither had he shot me yet. He looked quite young, early twenties probably, nervous eyes. Skin about two shades darker than mine. Rather handsome in a feminine sort of way. He didn't look crazy, just very wary. He walked up to within about ten feet of me.

"The Landrover—is empty?" Definitely a Cuban accent.

"Except for the money."

"Get in drive side. Very slow. Keep you hands where I see. If no, I shoot. Move."

There was a sheen of sweat on his hands. I hoped his finger didn't slip on the trigger—that damn thing looked like a cannon from where I was. He wasn't the only one who was sweating just then. I moved very carefully and slowly. He'd shoot if I so much as breathed crooked, I could see it in his eyes, but why did he want . . .? Oh, oh. We were going someplace else and Bobby would be left behind. I wondered how much it had hurt that calf to be killed that way and then made myself stop. Maybe we wouldn't go very far. Since he hadn't just taken the money and shot me, Ken must still be alive somewhere—wherever we were going. My earlier guess that he wanted me to see Ken die must've been right. That was what I'd been counting on, but I hadn't thought about his taking me away from the bridge. Why hadn't he brought Ken here to kill? The road was seldom used. Maybe he didn't know that.

I got in extremely carefully, keeping my hands up while he walked around, looked in the Landrover suspiciously, then climbed in. Kept the gun on me with one hand while he felt inside the bag with the other. He relaxed a bit when he pulled out a bundle of money.

"Good. Very good. Spoil plans you try trick. Very smart not try. Now drive."

Plans?? I drove as slowly as I dared to give Bobby as much time as possible. About two miles later the man told me to stop. I hoped my relief didn't show. I'd started to get really worried. Bobby would take awhile to make those two miles staying out of sight, but "plans" sounded like whatever our friend had in mind might take some time. He motioned me out and down a barely noticeable track leading away from the road. Very obliging of him to have me leave the Landrover beside the track so Bobby would know where we'd gone. Ten minutes walk led to an abandoned hut. Looked like part of a deserted logging camp. The shells of two other huts remained, as well as several bits of rusty metal that looked like they belonged to large machines at one time.

Easy to approach unseen. The man must've bought my solo arrival. He jerked the gun at me, apparently meaning for me to enter, so I opened the door and stepped in.

Ken lay in the corner bound and gagged but unquestionably alive. I don't believe I've ever felt so relieved in my life.

We were still a long ways from home, but Ken was alive and Bobby was on his way.

"Ken! Am I glad to see you!" That had to be the understatement of the year.

"Silent! Put money by door. Now untie you brother but I warn, you try anything, either you, I kill you both."

Ken untied as well?

I did as I was told. The rope was very tight and very professionally tied. I rubbed Ken's arms and legs for several minutes before he could stand up. . . . He grimaced but didn't speak. Neither did I. The atmosphere didn't lend itself to casual conversation.

"Sit on chair."

I looked around to see which of us he meant. Me. I sat down slowly. It was a crudely-fashioned chair and table. The man stood just inside the door. The room would have been dark except for the sunlight streaming in through several large gaps in the walls. Odds and ends lay on the floor. Dirty, cracked cups and a dented pan on the table. The man pulled a pair of handcuffs from a pocket, throwing them to Ken, who automatically tried to catch them but missed. They hit the dirt with a soft thud.

"Pick up. You put you sister right hand to back the chair." He waved the gun back and forth then shouted at me, "You let him or you die!"

Ken started to open his mouth but thought better of it. He put the handcuffs on instead. The metal felt oddly warm on my wrist—from the man's body heat, I supposed, or the sun while he was waiting at the bridge. The click of the lock was loud in the abandoned hut.

"Good. Now throw key my foot." Ken did so, slowly and carefully. "Good. Now take rope you tie with and tie she other hand to table front of she."

Ken looked confused but I wasn't—you can't remove fingernails easily if the hand is flailing around free. Again Ken did as he was told.

"Now tie feet chair also."

Trussed like a goddamn turkey and nothing to do about it except pray Bobby got here soon.

The man pulled out a knife, a small folding one, and tossed it to Ken. Oh God. He really was a sweetheart! Ken still hadn't connected—stood there holding the knife looking utterly bewildered.

"Take she clothes off." Huh? At least that wouldn't hurt and would give Bobby a few more minutes. Ken looked truly horrified for the first time since I'd entered the hut.

"But . . . but I can't do that! I . . ."

"You want you sister get she head blown off? You think she look better so?" The man giggled and pointed the gun at my head.

Ken took a long time about it until the man fired off a couple of rounds into the dirt inches from my feet. Fortunately dirt doesn't ricochet. Ken got the rest of my clothes off a lot faster. Once he muttered, "Sorry Sis." I said nothing. My clothes lay in pieces around the chair.

"Now you cut off she hair. Then you burn it, on floor."

God damn him, I'd never cut it in my life!

Ken looked like he couldn't believe what he'd heard. "What are you—crazy? Why should I do such a thing?"

I knew why—because it is humiliating and gets you used to the idea of doing violence to me! Bobby! Hurry up!—but I said nothing aloud. Ken was miles out of his depth. Farm life had never prepared him for confronting an insane, and obviously sadistic killer. Despite being kidnapped for days, he seemed to just now be beginning to realize how wrong things were. The man shouted.

"Do it! Quick. She no need she hair. Burn it. You do everything I tell you or I kill she." The gun jerked crazily back and forth, between us. Ken was suddenly convinced.

He tried to undo my bun and got all snarled up in the garrotte. I told him to just cut it off underneath instead of trying to undo it all. He must've thought the wire was just some contraption I used to keep my hair coiled properly. Eventually he got my hair sawed off. The gun motioned toward the box of matches lying on the floor beside a small camping stove. Ken laid my hair down and, with a long look at the man, struck a match to it. The smell of burning hair isn't particularly pleasant but the man looked like he enjoyed it. My hair burned down until it was just a smoldering pile of ash, which fortunately hid the wire. It would even still be usable, not that I foresaw any chance of using it.

Well, the man had about run out of non-painful things to do to me. I tried to brace myself for losing my fingernails. I kept picturing my Boss's hands and that didn't help at all. "Next you cut off she small finger. That you burn also. Gasoline can in corner. You pour on finger, light it. On table, so she see, see how she die."

Ken's jaw literally sagged and he made a small sick noise. My stomach heaved and I could feel the sudden sweat trickling down between my bare breasts. I had been somewhat prepared for losing some fingernails, but the possibility of losing a finger hadn't occurred to me. And I knew with nightmare certainty, that a man blood-crazy enough to deliver messages by gutting calves and decapitating cats wasn't going to stop with one finger. The table was rickety and lightweight—the thought of heaving it and myself across the small room nearly seduced me. But there'd be time for the gun to half empty itself and someone would get shot—and that someone would be Ken, who wouldn't have the sense to get out of the way. No, I had to trust Bobby to come soon. Then I realized the man was voicing my worst fears.

"But first you cut off all she other fingers, burn them. One a time."

Ken turned as if to run out of the hut but stopped when I screamed, "Ken! NO! You'll get us both killed!" The man was cursing him and threatening us both in Spanish, his English momentarily forgotten.

He stopped so I went on, giving the Cuban time to control his trigger finger, "Remember Sarah and the children. You better do what the man says."

About that time the man got his English back. "You do I tell you! You live. And you wife and you childs. Besides, I have tell you of the crimes you sister have made. She must die for them. But she must hurt first. She feel flames here, then she feel them in Hell. See? Even she know how terrible she crimes—why she tell you do this thing to she if she no know?"

I disagreed with that and said so—besides, as long as we were talking I wasn't getting chopped up. I didn't say I knew he intended to kill Ken after he'd had his fun burning me piece by piece. I had to gain time for Bobby so I asked, "What crimes? Are you crazy or something?"

"I crazy, yes! I crazy with pain for my love you torture. Now is you turn, you have much pain, much pain more than he!"

Love? That I'd tortured?? Then it all fell into place. He was

Guiterra's lover. Guiterra hadn't stayed true to his political lover, but had had this young thug on the side. The thought of anyone, man or woman, who could love Guiterra was unbelievable. But here was one lamenting him and planning on making me pay for his death in a particularly grisly fashion. Burning was the one death I couldn't bear even the thought of. But Bobby would come. He had to. Hang in there till he comes. You've managed before— you can again. But it hadn't been by fire before. Stop it. It's the knife you'll feel not the fire. Bobby will come long long before that. The man obviously wants this to last so Bobby will have plenty of time. You've survived knives before. Then I shut out my mind's whimperings. I couldn't afford to hear them.

I tried insulting Guiterra in an effort to delay the proceedings but he wouldn't bite. Just told Ken to get a move on if he wanted to see his family again. I wished desperately that I could tell Ken the situation wasn't as bad as it looked, not that I was feeling any too cheerful about it just then. What an inhumanly hideous choice, torture your sister, or die and know your family will too!

"Go on Ken. You have no choice so don't think about it." Couldn't believe I managed to say such crap. If it had been *me* standing free with a knife, it would have been that young punk who bled, not a member of my family! But Ken hadn't had the benefit of years of Bobby's training, so I couldn't expect anything of him.

It took a long time. The knife was dull. The more Ken tried not to hurt, the more he did. Would've been a lot easier on both of us if he'd sawed as hard and fast as possible but he didn't. Nor did I suggest he should. The longer he took, the closer Bobby would be before he had to do the next one. Ten fingers would take a long time. I couldn't face the thought of losing the use of my hands. Even the Boss has some use of his. I can't lose my hands. I can't! Stop. Put it away—don't think of the future now. Then the pain was far too bad to let me think about anything else. With incredible clarity I saw a drop of sweat fall from Ken's face to mingle with the blood that was seeping across the table. My hand seemed to have a life of its own, jerking and twisting to get away. I stared at it. Looked at Ken once and wished I hadn't.

Pain. Pain is a strange thing. No matter how much you've experienced you never become immune to it. You know it's been as bad before, and it ended, but after a point you cannot believe it will end this time. Seconds stretch into vast universes of time. Each second you survive is a victory. That is the only way you can allow yourself to feel. Each second is another victory. The first ones are the worst. If you can last enough seconds, thousands upon thousands of seconds one after another, it suddenly becomes easier. Even when you pass out and they drag you back to face the pain again. For days or weeks. Until either the body or the mind has had all it can take. Then the victim dies, goes irreparably insane or breaks. At least this time no one was asking me for information. And it wouldn't last that long—it couldn't. Oh God, it couldn't! Not again!

No! Never, never think of the pain yet to come. Just survive what is there at the moment. It felt like every nerve in my body was being amputated, not just one finger. How could it take so long to remove such a small bone? The blood was running over the edge of the table and I could hear it dripping on the floor.

When the finger finally came off, Ken just stood there looking at it. The man stopped laughing and told him to get the gasoline and burn it. When he spoke, I realized he'd been laughing the whole time.

Ken moved like a sleepwalker as he got the can and carried it to the table. He stared at the finger, then gingerly pushed it out of the blood before he poured gas over it. The vapor lit before the match ever touched, making him jump back.

The smell as the flesh began to burn was utterly nauseating. The finger, my finger, jerked in the flames, not knowing it was dead yet. My hand was still trying to crawl away from the pain too. I couldn't look away from the flames and the blackened thing they fed on, even when I heard Ken vomiting. I sat rigid, unable to vomit or scream or do anything but watch.

Eventually the flames died and the man waved his gun around until Ken started on the next finger. He was shaking so badly he could barely hold the knife. He stank of vomit, though how I could smell it over the other stench, I don't know. He couldn't make two cuts in the same place. The harder he tried, the worse he shook. My ring finger was rapidly resembling hamburger. The man seemed to think he'd never seen anything so funny before in his life. I watched the knife from miles away across an ocean of pain. It was better than looking at the black thing on the table.

A shadow flickered at the farthest edge of my vision. Hope and adrenaline surged as I forced myself not to move—praying the shadow was Bobby. Was that . . . YES!! YES!! I didn't dare look directly in case I warned the Cuban. But I could see Bobby's arm and a gleam of metal as he smashed the heavy handle of his knife against the side of the Cuban's ear.

I looked up as he spoke to Ken, saying, "You can stop butchering Tessa now."

"Bobby! Christ but you took your own sweet time gett'n here!" My speech was so pain-slurred I could hardly understand myself. And I wondered at the absurd self image that speaks such words when all I really wanted to do was cry.

Ken stared at Bobby as if he'd come from another planet. Bobby checked the Cuban, then reversed his knife and slid it back in its sheath as he said, "How about you use that pigsticker and cut Tessa loose, huh? 'Stead of just standing there. Least I assume you must be the brother 'n not a friend of his." Bobby gestured at the unconscious figure on the floor. Ken didn't move so Bobby took the knife from him and cut my hand free.

"Key to my handcuffs is on the floor somewhere beside the body." At least that's what I tried to say, but it came out more like a whimper.

"Soon as I stop you from bleed'n to death." Bobby very gently bandaged my hand after digging a first aid kit out of his sack. Then he undid the handcuffs and untied my legs. Ken never moved or spoke. I was suddenly acutely aware of being naked. Bobby must've seen my discomfort because he gave me his shirt and helped me put it on. Finally he looked at what was left of my finger and then at me.

"What you want ta do with it?"

"I don't know." I stared at it in utter revulsion. Charred and cracked and still smoking slightly, a piece of white bone showed at the end nearest me. It didn't look like a finger. It looked obscene. The stench in the hut and the pain were making my head swim and my stomach churn. I couldn't make myself think about Bobby's question. Dimly I heard him say, "Okay, I'll bury it once I get done. Meanwhile you better take your brother outside while I find out the score from this joker."

I tried to stand up and nearly passed out. Bobby grabbed me and steadied me until I could stand. His worried face helped me pull myself together enough to walk outside. Ken followed slowly. The sun felt hot and good.

We were nearly to the Landrover before we heard the first scream. I started shaking and couldn't stop. Ken patted my shoulder rather uncertainly. We walked on. The pain blurred my vision and made walking misery. Bobby'd made a makeshift sling for my hand and now it bumped against my chest with each step. Tried holding it with my other hand but that hurt worse. Ken spoke finally.

"Was . . . was there anything I shoulda done?"

"No."

After a moment Ken said "Tessa. I . . . I'm sorry. I didn't know you had a . . . friend outside when I chose my family 'stead of you. I . . . I hope you understand. I'da cut my own finger off if I coulda, but I couldn't let anything happen to the kids."

I wondered how much that had influenced him, and how much had been just plain fear—then wished I hadn't thought that. So I made myself say, "I know. Forget it—it's over, both of us are alive and so is your family. It could've been much much worse. If he'd had a chance to finish what he started, he'd've killed us both and your family anyway. If I was in any other line of work it would never've happened."

The Landrover came in sight before either of us spoke again. "Did you torture his friend?"

"Yes. Not for kicks though." He didn't say anything so I asked "Why?"

"He talked a lot 'bout how you killed his people. More 'bout how you tortured his friend. Made you out to be a very cruel person." Ken stopped walking and gave me a look I'll remember a long time. "He was pretty convincing."

The words hurt a long way inside. Perhaps I should have told him some of what Guiterra had done to his victims over the years. Perhaps I should have explained about a kid still in a hospital because he borrowed my karabiner. I could have pointed out that Ken had just done a bit of torture himself because of the situation he'd been in. There were a lot of things I might've said. Instead I heard myself talking about a calf and a cat and a lot of blood—and a woman beyond even fear, finally, who'd cried all night. Ken turned white as the proverbial sheet and didn't speak again.

The sun was bright, the air hot and muggy. Sweat soaked through my borrowed shirt and puddled under my legs on the plastic seat of the Landrover. My hand throbbed viciously. Flies buzzed around the bandages. Obscene blue flies crawling over blood-soaked gauze covering an obscene wound. The minutes crawled like the flies. I closed my eyes but the glare off the hood glowed redly through my eyelids. Ken sat, unmoving, on the roadside, as if he couldn't bear to be near me. He looked sick and old. Doubted I'd win any beauty contests either just then. Looked up the track for the hundredth time. This time Bobby was there, running lightly and easily. He reached the Landrover and swung the money and his pack into the back. Ken came over slowly and climbed into the back too. He didn't seem to think much of our company.

Bobby got into the driver's seat. "Everything's okay. Your friend was the last of Guiterra's lot. Seems 'e got knocked out 'n left for dead when you blew up the cave. Unfortunately, 'e didn' stay dead. Came to sometime the next day. Found several bodies but not Guiterra's. Seemed obsessed about finding him. Finally saw tracks go'n into a gravel pit and followed them. Gather you did a good job on Guiterra. Anyway, 'e buried what the vultures'd left and hung around. Long story, but 'e finally tracked you to your brother's farm, but you'd left by then to go sailing with your niece. 'E didn't know if you was even in the country still so 'e hit on the idea of kidnapping Ken. Figured Sarah'd know where you was and get in touch. The rest you know. 'E didn't even know how to contact Havana! That's why 'e wanted money—didn't have the price of a bleed'n plane ticket! Had dreams a goin' back to Havana a great hero. 'E can dream all 'e likes now. How'sa hand?"

"Hurts. Sounds like we can go home."

AUTHOR'S NOTE

BELIZE, the country, is real, as are its road system, cities, hotels, etc. So, too, is Airport Camp, though its security is now much tighter than when I first wrote this book. Strictly for purposes of this story, I have chosen to leave its security measures years out of date. The Hummingbird Lumber Company does not exist, although Caves Branch River and the old sawmill do. Mountain Cow Cave is as beautiful as ever, not having been blown up in real life, as it is in these pages.

All characters, as well as the World Council for Human Rights, the Watchdog Organization, and Papacito's, are fictitious and do not represent any real persons or organizations.

ACKNOWLEDGMENTS

FIRST AND FOREMOST, my gratitude to Jonnie (Erma J.) Fisk, a published author who was willing to help get someone else's work published and who spent many hours trying to teach me how to create 3-D characters. Without Jonnie, this book would still be on the back shelf of my closet.

Also, I wish to thank Paul and Sheila Langston-Greene, who gave me house space while I wrote the first draft, and Martin Lowe, who taught me to climb and who regularly dragged me away from my typewriter to go climbing or target shooting.

I would also like to thank all the people from the Wigan Rifle Club and British Forces Belize whom I've pestered for technical information.